GENOCIDE & PERSECUTION

The People's
Republic of China

Titles in the Genocide and Persecution Series

GENOCIDE & PERSECUTION

The People's Republic of China

Jeff Hay
Book Editor

Frank Chalk
Consulting Editor

GREENHAVEN PRESS
A part of Gale, Cengage Learning

GALE
CENGAGE Learning·

Detroit • New York • San Francisco • New Haven, Conn • Waterville, Maine • London

Elizabeth Des Chenes, *Director, Publishing Solutions*

For more information, contact:
Greenhaven Press
27500 Drake Rd.
Farmington Hills, MI 48331-3535
Or you can visit our Internet site at gale.cengage.com.

For product information and technology assistance, contact us at:

Gale Customer Support, 1-800-877-4253
For permission to use material from this text or product, submit all requests online at www.cengage.com/permissions

Further permissions questions can be emailed to permissionrequest@cengage.com

Every effort is made to ensure that Greenhaven Press accurately reflects the original intent of the authors. Every effort has been made to trace the owners of copyrighted material.

Cover image © Bettmann/CORBIS.
Interior barbed wire artwork © f9photos, used under license from Shutterstock.com.

LIBRARY OF CONGRESS CATALOGING-IN-PUBLICATION DATA

The People's Republic of China / Jeff Hay, book editor.
   p. cm. -- (Genocide and persecution)
   Includes bibliographical references and index.
   ISBN 978-0-7377-6253-2 (hbk.)
1. Political persecution--China--History. 2. Human rights--China--History. 3. Civil rights--China--History. 4. Genocide--China--History. 5. China--History--Cultural Revolution, 1966-1976. 6. China--Politics and government--20th century. 7. China --Politics and government--21st century. 8. China--Social conditions--20th century. 9. China--Social conditions--21st century.
I. Hay, Jeff.
   JC599.C6P46 2012
   323.4'90951--dc23
                                                                    2012011592

Printed in the United States of America
1 2 3 4 5 6 7 16 15 14 13 12

Contents

Chapter 1: Historical Background on the People's Republic of China

Red Guards, made up of high school and university student activists, were the foot soldiers of the Cultural Revolution. In early 1967 groups of Red Guards in the Chinese capital of Beijing issued a statement in which, among other ambitions, they promised to destroy opponents of the Revolution.

Chapter 2: Controversies Surrounding the People's Republic of China

A Chinese official argues before the National People's Committee that the crackdown in Tiananmen Square was necessary to stop anti-government activity stirred up, in part, by foreigners.

Chapter 3: Personal Narratives

Preface

The histories of many nations are shaped by horrific events involving torture, violent repression, and systematic mass killings. The inhumanity of such events is difficult to comprehend, yet understanding why such events take place, what impact they have on society, and how they may be prevented in the future is vitally important. The Genocide and Persecution series provides readers with anthologies of previously published materials on acts of genocide, crimes against humanity, and other instances of extreme persecution, with an emphasis on events taking place in the twentieth and twenty-first centuries. The series offers essential historical background on these significant events in modern world history, presents the issues and controversies surrounding the events, and provides first-person narratives from people whose lives were altered by the events. By providing primary sources, as well as analysis of crucial issues, these volumes help develop critical-thinking skills and support global connections. In addition, the series directly addresses curriculum standards focused on informational text and literary nonfiction and explicitly promotes literacy in history and social studies.

Each Genocide and Persecution volume focuses on genocide, crimes against humanity, or severe persecution. Material from a variety of primary and secondary sources presents a multinational perspective on the event. Articles are carefully edited and introduced to provide context for readers. The series includes volumes on significant and widely studied events like the Holocaust, as well as events that are less often studied, such as the East Pakistan genocide in what is now Bangladesh. Some volumes focus on multiple events endured by a specific people, such as the Kurds, or multiple events enacted over time by a particular oppressor or in a particular location, such as the People's Republic of China.

Each volume is organized into three chapters. The first chapter provides readers with general background information and uses primary sources such as testimony from tribunals or international courts, documents or speeches from world leaders, and legislative text. The second chapter presents multinational perspectives on issues and controversies and addresses current implications or long-lasting effects of the event. Viewpoints explore such topics as root causes; outside interventions, if any; the impact on the targeted group and the region; and the contentious issues that arose in the aftermath. The third chapter presents first-person narratives from affected people, including survivors, family members of victims, perpetrators, officials, aid workers, and other witnesses.

In addition, numerous features are included in each volume of Genocide and Persecution:

- An annotated **table of contents** provides a brief summary of each essay in the volume.
- A **foreword** gives important background information on the recognition, definition, and study of genocide in recent history and examines current efforts focused on the prevention of future atrocities.
- A **chronology** offers important dates leading up to, during, and following the event.
- **Primary sources**—including historical newspaper accounts, testimony, and personal narratives—are among the varied selections in the anthology.
- **Illustrations**—including a world map, photographs, charts, graphs, statistics, and tables—are closely tied

to the text and chosen to help readers understand key points or concepts.

- **Sidebars**—including biographies of key figures and overviews of earlier or related historical events—offer additional content.
- **Pedagogical features**—including analytical exercises, writing prompts, and group activities—introduce each chapter and help reinforce the material. These features promote proficiency in writing, speaking, and listening skills and literacy in history and social studies.
- A **glossary** defines key terms, as needed.
- An annotated list of international **organizations to contact** presents sources of additional information on the volume topic.
- A **list of primary source documents** provides an annotated list of reports, treaties, resolutions, and judicial decisions related to the volume topic.
- A **for further research** section offers a bibliography of books, periodical articles, and Internet sources and an annotated section of other items such as films and websites.
- A comprehensive subject **index** provides access to key people, places, events, and subjects cited in the text.

The Genocide and Persecution series illuminates atrocities that cannot and should not be forgotten. By delving deeply into these events from a variety of perspectives, students and other readers are provided with the information they need to think critically about the past and its implications for the future.

Foreword

The term *genocide* often appears in news stories and other literature. It is not widely known, however, that the core meaning of the term comes from a legal definition, and the concept became part of international criminal law only in 1951 when the United Nations Convention on the Prevention and Punishment of the Crime of Genocide came into force. The word *genocide* appeared in print for the first time in 1944 when Raphael Lemkin, a Polish Jewish refugee from Adolf Hitler's World War II invasion of Eastern Europe, invented the term and explored its meaning in his pioneering book *Axis Rule in Occupied Europe.*

Humanity's Recognition of Genocide and Persecution

Lemkin understood that throughout the history of the human race there have always been leaders who thought they could solve their problems not only through victory in war, but also by destroying entire national, ethnic, racial, or religious groups. Such annihilations of entire groups, in Lemkin's view, deprive the world of the very cultural diversity and richness in languages, traditions, values, and practices that distinguish the human race from all other life on earth. Genocide is not only unjust, it threatens the very existence and progress of human civilization, in Lemkin's eyes.

Looking to the past, Lemkin understood that the prevailing coarseness and brutality of earlier human societies and the lower value placed on human life obscured the existence of genocide. Sacrifice and exploitation, as well as torture and public execution, had been common at different times in history. Looking toward a more humane future, Lemkin asserted the need to punish—and when possible prevent—a crime for which there had been no name until he invented it.

Legal Definitions of Genocide

On December 9, 1948, the United Nations adopted its Convention on the Prevention and Punishment of the Crime of Genocide (UNGC). Under Article II, genocide

> means any of the following acts committed with intent to destroy, in whole or in part, a national, ethnical, racial or religious group, as such:
>
> (a) Killing members of the group;
>
> (b) Causing serious bodily or mental harm to members of the group;
>
> (c) Deliberately inflicting on the group conditions of life calculated to bring about its physical destruction in whole or in part;
>
> (d) Imposing measures intended to prevent births within the group;
>
> (e) Forcibly transferring children of the group to another group.

Article III of the convention defines the elements of the crime of genocide, making punishable:

> (a) Genocide;
>
> (b) Conspiracy to commit genocide;
>
> (c) Direct and public incitement to commit genocide;
>
> (d) Attempt to commit genocide;
>
> (e) Complicity in genocide.

After intense debate, the architects of the convention excluded acts committed with intent to destroy social, political, and economic groups from the definition of genocide. Thus, attempts to destroy whole social classes—the physically and mentally challenged, and homosexuals, for example—are not acts of genocide under the terms of the UNGC. These groups achieved a belated but very significant measure of protection under international criminal law in the Rome Statute of the International Criminal

Court, adopted at a conference on July 17, 1998, and entered into force on July 1, 2002.

The Rome Statute defined a crime against humanity in the following way:

> any of the following acts when committed as part of a widespread and systematic attack directed against any civilian population:
>
> (a) Murder;
>
> (b) Extermination;
>
> (c) Enslavement;
>
> (d) Deportation or forcible transfer of population;
>
> (e) Imprisonment or other severe deprivation of physical liberty in violation of fundamental rules of international law;
>
> (f) Torture;
>
> (g) Rape, sexual slavery, enforced prostitution, forced pregnancy, enforced sterilization, or any other form of sexual violence of comparable gravity;
>
> (h) Persecution against any identifiable group or collectivity on political, racial, national, ethnic, cultural, religious, gender . . . or other grounds that are universally recognized as impermissible under international law, in connection with any act referred to in this paragraph or any crime within the jurisdiction of this Court;
>
> (i) Enforced disappearance of persons;
>
> (j) The crime of apartheid;
>
> (k) Other inhumane acts of a similar character intentionally causing great suffering, or serious injury to body or to mental or physical health.

Although genocide is often ranked as "the crime of crimes," in practice prosecutors find it much easier to convict perpetrators of crimes against humanity rather than genocide under domestic laws. However, while Article I of the UNGC declares that countries adhering to the UNGC recognize genocide as "a crime under international law which they undertake to prevent and to punish," the Rome Statute provides no comparable international mechanism for the prosecution of crimes against humanity. A treaty would help individual countries and international institutions introduce measures to prevent crimes against humanity, as well as open more avenues to the domestic and international prosecution of war criminals.

The Evolving Laws of Genocide

In the aftermath of the serious crimes committed against civilians in the former Yugoslavia since 1991 and the Rwanda genocide of 1994, the United Nations Security Council created special international courts to bring the alleged perpetrators of these events to justice. While the UNGC stands as the standard definition of genocide in law, the new courts contributed significantly to today's nuanced meaning of genocide, crimes against humanity, ethnic cleansing, and serious war crimes in international criminal law.

Also helping to shape contemporary interpretations of such mass atrocity crimes are the special and mixed courts for Sierra Leone, Cambodia, Lebanon, and Iraq, which may be the last of their type in light of the creation of the International Criminal Court (ICC), with its broad jurisdiction over mass atrocity crimes in all countries that adhere to the Rome Statute of the ICC. The Yugoslavia and Rwanda tribunals have already clarified the law of genocide, ruling that rape can be prosecuted as a weapon in committing genocide, evidence of intent can be absent when convicting low-level perpetrators of genocide, and public incitement to commit genocide is a crime even if genocide does not immediately follow the incitement.

Several current controversies about genocide are worth noting and will require more research in the future:

1. Dictators accused of committing genocide or persecution may hold onto power more tightly for fear of becoming

vulnerable to prosecution after they step down. Therefore, do threats of international indictments of these alleged perpetrators actually delay transfers of power to more representative rulers, thereby causing needless suffering?

2. Would the large sum of money spent for international retributive justice be better spent on projects directly benefiting the survivors of genocide and persecution?

3. Can international courts render justice impartially or do they deliver only "victors' justice," that is the application of one set of rules to judge the vanquished and a different and laxer set of rules to judge the victors?

It is important to recognize that the law of genocide is constantly evolving, and scholars searching for the roots and early warning signs of genocide may prefer to use their own definitions of genocide in their work. While the UNGC stands as the standard definition of genocide in law, the debate over its interpretation and application will never end. The ultimate measure of the value of any definition of genocide is its utility for identifying the roots of genocide and preventing future genocides.

Motives for Genocide and Early Warning Signs

When identifying past cases of genocide, many scholars work with some version of the typology of motives published in 1990 by historian Frank Chalk and sociologist Kurt Jonassohn in their book *The History and Sociology of Genocide*. The authors identify the following four motives and acknowledge that they may overlap, or several lesser motives might also drive a perpetrator:

1. To eliminate a real or potential threat, as in Imperial Rome's decision to annihilate Carthage in 146 BC.

2. To spread terror among real or potential enemies, as in Genghis Khan's destruction of city-states and people who rebelled against the Mongols in the thirteenth century.

3. To acquire economic wealth, as in the case of the Massachusetts Puritans' annihilation of the native Pequot people in 1637.

4. To implement a belief, theory, or an ideology, as in the case of Germany's decision under Hitler and the Nazis to destroy completely the Jewish people of Europe from 1941 to 1945.

Although these motives represent differing goals, they share common early warning signs of genocide. A good example of genocide in recent times that could have been prevented through close attention to early warning signs was the genocide of 1994 inflicted on the people labeled as "Tutsi" in Rwanda. Between 1959 and 1963, the predominantly Hutu political parties in power stigmatized all Tutsi as members of a hostile racial group, violently forcing their leaders and many civilians into exile in neighboring countries through a series of assassinations and massacres. Despite systematic exclusion of Tutsi from service in the military, government security agencies, and public service, as well as systematic discrimination against them in higher education, hundreds of thousands of Tutsi did remain behind in Rwanda. Government-issued cards identified each Rwandan as Hutu or Tutsi.

A generation later, some Tutsi raised in refugee camps in Uganda and elsewhere joined together, first organizing politically and then militarily, to reclaim a place in their homeland. When the predominantly Tutsi Rwanda Patriotic Front invaded Rwanda from Uganda in October 1990, extremist Hutu political parties demonized all of Rwanda's Tutsi as traitors, ratcheting up hate propaganda through radio broadcasts on government-run Radio Rwanda and privately owned radio station RTLM. Within the print media, *Kangura* and other publications used vicious cartoons to further demonize Tutsi and to stigmatize any Hutu who dared advocate bringing Tutsi into the government. Massacres of dozens and later hundreds of Tutsi sprang up even as Rwandans prepared to elect a coalition government led by moderate political parties, and as the United Nations dispatched a small international military force led by Canadian general Roméo Dallaire to oversee the elections and political transition. Late in 1992, an international human rights organization's investigating team detected the hate propaganda campaign, verified systematic massacres of Tutsi, and warned the international community that Rwanda had already entered the early stages of genocide, to no avail. On April 6, 1994, Rwanda's genocidal killing accelerated at an alarming pace when someone shot down the airplane flying Rwandan president Juvenal Habyarimana home from peace talks in Arusha, Tanzania.

Hundreds of thousands of Tutsi civilians—including children, women, and the elderly—died horrible deaths because the world ignored the early warning signs of the genocide and refused to act. Prominent among those early warning signs were: 1) systematic, government-decreed discrimination against the Tutsi as members of a supposed racial group; 2) government-issued identity cards labeling every Tutsi as a member of a racial group; 3) hate propaganda casting all Tutsi as subversives and traitors; 4) organized assassinations and massacres targeting Tutsi; and 5) indoctrination of militias and special military units to believe that all Tutsi posed a genocidal threat to the existence of Hutu and would enslave Hutu if they ever again became the rulers of Rwanda.

Genocide Prevention and the Responsibility to Protect

The shock waves emanating from the Rwanda genocide forced world leaders at least to acknowledge in principle that the national sovereignty of offending nations cannot trump the responsibility of those governments to prevent the infliction of mass atrocities on their own people. When governments violate that obligation, the member states of the United Nations have a responsibility to get involved. Such involvement can take the form of, first, offering to help the local government change its ways through technical advice and development aid, and second—if the local government persists in assaulting its own people—initiating armed intervention to protect the civilians at risk. In 2005 the United Nations began to implement the Responsibility to Protect initiative, a framework of principles to guide the international community in preventing mass atrocities.

As in many real-world domains, theory and practice often diverge. Genocide and crimes against humanity are rooted in problems that produce failing states: poverty, poor education, extreme nationalism, lawlessness, dictatorship, and corruption. Implementing the principles of the Responsibility to Protect doctrine burdens intervening state leaders with the necessity of addressing each of those problems over a long period of time. And when those problems prove too intractable and complex to solve easily, the citizens of the intervening nations may lose patience, voting out the leader who initiated the intervention. Arguments based solely on humanitarian principles fail to overcome such concerns. What is needed to persuade political leaders to stop preventable mass atrocities are compelling arguments based on their own national interests.

Preventable mass atrocities threaten the national interests of all states in five specific ways:

1. Mass atrocities create conditions that engender widespread and concrete threats from terrorism, piracy, and other forms of lawlessness on the land and sea;
2. Mass atrocities facilitate the spread of warlordism, whose tentacles block affordable access to vital raw materials produced in the affected country and threaten the prosperity of all nations that depend on the consumption of these resources;
3. Mass atrocities trigger cascades of refugees and internally displaced populations that, combined with climate change and growing international air travel, will accelerate the worldwide incidence of lethal infectious diseases;

4. Mass atrocities spawn single-interest parties and political agendas that drown out more diverse political discourse in the countries where the atrocities take place and in the countries that host large numbers of refugees. Xenophobia and nationalist backlashes are the predictable consequences of government indifference to mass atrocities elsewhere that could have been prevented through early actions;

5. Mass atrocities foster the spread of national and transnational criminal networks trafficking in drugs, women, arms, contraband, and laundered money.

Alerting elected political representatives to the consequences of mass atrocities should be part of every student movement's agenda in the twenty-first century. Adam Smith, the great political economist and author of *The Wealth of Nations*, put it best when he wrote: "It is not from the benevolence of the butcher, the brewer, or the baker that we expect our dinner, but from their regard to their own interest." Self-interest is a powerful engine for good in the marketplace and can be an equally powerful motive and source of inspiration for state action to prevent genocide and mass persecution. In today's new global village, the lives we save may be our own.

Frank Chalk

Frank Chalk, who has a doctorate from the University of Wisconsin-Madison, is a professor of history and director of the Montreal Institute for Genocide and Human Rights Studies at Concordia University in Montreal, Canada. He is coauthor, with Kurt

Jonassohn, of The History and Sociology of Genocide *(1990); coauthor with General Roméo Dallaire, Kyle Matthews, Carla Barqueiro, and Simon Doyle of* Mobilizing the Will to Intervene: Leadership to Prevent Mass Atrocities *(2010); and associate editor of the three-volume Macmillan Reference USA* Encyclopedia of Genocide and Crimes Against Humanity *(2004). Chalk served as president of the International Association of Genocide Scholars from June 1999 to June 2001. His current research focuses on the use of radio and television broadcasting in the incitement and prevention of genocide, and domestic laws on genocide. For more information on genocide and examples of the experiences of people displaced by genocide and other human rights violations, interested readers can consult the websites of the Montreal Institute for Genocide and Human Rights Studies (http://migs.concordia.ca) and the Montreal Life Stories project (www.lifestoriesmontreal.ca).*

World Map

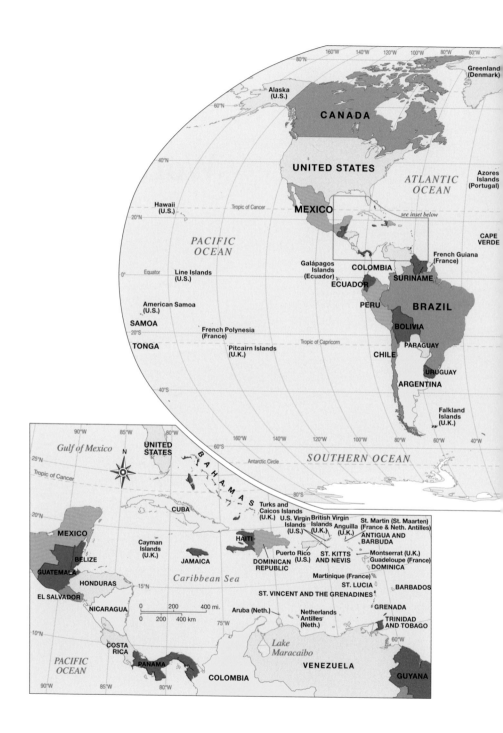

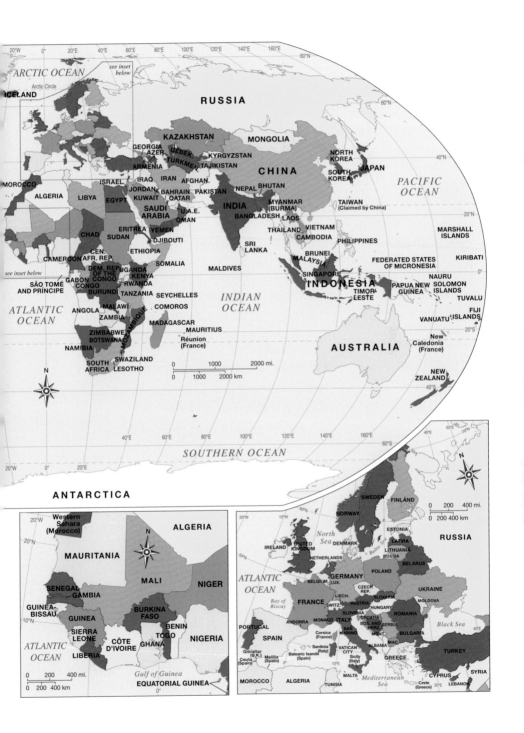

ARCTIC OCEAN
Arctic Circle
ICELAND
see inset below

RUSSIA

60°N

KAZAKHSTAN
MONGOLIA
GEORGIA
AZER. UZBEK.
KYRGYZSTAN
NORTH KOREA
40°N
ARMENIA TURKMEN. TAJIKISTAN
CHINA
SOUTH KOREA
JAPAN

MOROCCO
ISRAEL
IRAQ IRAN AFGHAN.
PACIFIC OCEAN
ALGERIA
LIBYA
EGYPT
JORDAN BAHRAIN PAKISTAN
KUWAIT QATAR
NEPAL BHUTAN
MYANMAR (BURMA)
TAIWAN (Claimed by China)
20°N
SAUDI ARABIA
U.A.E.
OMAN
INDIA
BANGLADESH LAOS

ERITREA YEMEN
THAILAND VIETNAM
MARSHALL ISLANDS
CHAD SUDAN
DJIBOUTI
CAMBODIA PHILIPPINES
CEN. AFR. REP. ETHIOPIA
SRI LANKA
CAMEROON
SOMALIA
BRUNEI
FEDERATED STATES OF MICRONESIA
KIRIBATI
see inset below
DEM. REP. UGANDA
OF THE CONGO KENYA
MALAYSIA
MALDIVES
SINGAPORE
NAURU
SÃO TOMÉ AND PRÍNCIPE
GABON CONGO RWANDA
BURUNDI TANZANIA SEYCHELLES
INDONESIA
TIMOR-LESTE
PAPUA NEW GUINEA
SOLOMON ISLANDS
0°
TUVALU

ATLANTIC OCEAN
ANGOLA MALAWI
ZAMBIA
COMOROS
INDIAN OCEAN
FIJI ISLANDS
VANUATU

MADAGASCAR
MAURITIUS
20°S
ZIMBABWE
BOTSWANA
Réunion (France)
AUSTRALIA
New Caledonia (France)
NAMIBIA
SWAZILAND
SOUTH AFRICA LESOTHO
0   1000   2000 mi.
0 1000 2000 km
NEW ZEALAND
40°S

SOUTHERN OCEAN

ANTARCTICA

Africa inset:
Western Sahara (Morocco)
ALGERIA
MAURITANIA
MALI
NIGER
SENEGAL
GAMBIA
GUINEA-BISSAU
GUINEA
BURKINA FASO
SIERRA LEONE
CÔTE D'IVOIRE
BENIN
TOGO
GHANA
NIGERIA
ATLANTIC OCEAN
LIBERIA
Gulf of Guinea
EQUATORIAL GUINEA
0   200   400 mi.
0 200 400 km

Europe inset:
SWEDEN FINLAND
NORWAY
North Sea
ESTONIA
RUSSIA
IRELAND UNITED KINGDOM DENMARK
LATVIA
LITHUANIA
RUSSIA
NETHERLANDS
BELARUS
POLAND
ATLANTIC OCEAN
BELGIUM LUX.
GERMANY
UKRAINE
CZECH REP.
Bay of Biscay
FRANCE
LIECH.
SWITZ. AUSTRIA
SLOVAKIA
HUNGARY
MOLDOVA
SLOVENIA
ROMANIA
ANDORRA MONACO ITALY
CROATIA
BOS. AND HERZ. SERBIA
Black Sea
PORTUGAL
SAN MARINO
MONT.
BULGARIA
SPAIN
Corsica (France)
VATICAN CITY
ALBANIA MAC.
Sardinia (Italy)
Sicily (Italy)
GREECE
TURKEY
Gibraltar (U.K.)
Ceuta (Spain)
Melilla (Spain)
Balearic Isands (Spain)
MALTA
CYPRUS
SYRIA
MOROCCO
ALGERIA
TUNISIA
Mediterranean Sea
Crete (Greece)
LEBANON
0   200   400 mi.
0 200 400 km

17

Chronology

1929	The Communist Party of China is formed.
1934	The Long March takes place, in which Mao Zedong and other leaders expand their support in the Chinese countryside.
1937–1945	China and Japan engage in the Second Sino-Japanese War.
1945–1949	The Chinese Communists and the nationalist Kuomintang engage in civil war.
1949	On October 1, Mao Zedong proclaims the founding of the People's Republic of China in Beijing's Tiananmen Square.
1958–1962	During the Great Leap Forward, heavy-handed attempts at economic development result in the deaths of millions by famine, imprisonment, and violence.
1959	China's People's Liberation Army quells a major rebellion in Tibet, cementing the region as a province of the People's Republic.
1961–1964	The Great Leap Forward slowly draws to a close as Mao temporarily loses influence.
1966–1976	During the Cultural Revolution, attempts by a revived Mao Zedong to create a uniform "revolutionary culture" throughout China result in violence against dissenters and ethnic minorities.

1976	On September 9, Mao Zedong dies, resulting in a power struggle over who would succeed him as China's leader.
1978	Deng Xiaoping, having emerged as China's leading official, begins a series of economic reforms based on the "four modernizations" of industry, agriculture, science, and defense.
1979	After three decades of tension, the People's Republic and the United States enter into formal diplomatic relations.
1986	Students stage the first demonstrations of the burgeoning pro-democracy movement.
April 15, 1989	Hu Yaobang, a high official deposed in 1987 for his readiness to accept political reforms, dies. Students begin gathering in Tiananmen Square to commemorate him.
April 27, 1989	Students from more than forty universities go to Beijing to participate in the demonstrations taking place in Tiananmen Square.
May 20, 1989	The government declares martial law to quell the continuing demonstrations in Beijing. These now include hunger strikes and the formation of would-be labor unions.
June 3–4, 1989	People's Liberation Army commanders in Beijing receive orders to clear Tiananmen Square. Although accounts differ, negotiated agreements lead most

demonstrators to leave the Square over-
night or in the early morning hours, but
violence results in injuries and fatalities.

1993   At a human rights conference in Vienna,
            Austria, a Chinese diplomat asserts that
            human rights must take second place to
            China's economic development.

1997   Riots break out among Uighurs in
            China's Xinjiang province on the occa-
            sion of Deng Xiaoping's death.

2008   Beijing hosts the 2008 Summer Olympic
            Games.

2009   Riots and demonstrations in Urumqi, the
            capital of Uighur-dominated Xinjiang
            province, leave hundreds killed and
            injured.

2010   China becomes the world's second-
            largest economy.

2011   Ethnic demonstrations turn into riots
            in China's northern Lower Mongolia
            region.

CHAPTER 1

Historical Background on the People's Republic of China

Chapter Exercises

1. Analyzing Statistics

Question 1: Examine the statistics on Chinese ethnic groups. Do you think the percentage of Han Chinese is large enough compared to other groups to be able to dominate the country? How would members of ethnic minorities challenge attempts at domination?

Question 2: China's GDP (gross domestic product) indicates that China now has the world's second largest economy (of any individual country) after the United States. How has China's focus on economic growth influenced its policies and the general attitude of leaders toward human rights?

Question 3: China's population is the largest in the world. How does the total number compare with those in other large countries such as the United States, India, or Brazil, or rich but smaller ones such as Japan or Germany? What role has the large population played in the policies of China's government?

2. Writing Prompt

Write an article analyzing the Great Leap Forward. Give it a strong title that will grab readers' attention. Be sure to examine such questions as the intentions of China's leaders in starting agricultural and industrial reforms as well as the human costs of these changes. Identify specific leaders, specific reforms, and the time frame in which the event took place.

3. Group Activity

Form into small groups and examine the Great Leap Forward, the Cultural Revolution, the Tiananmen Square crackdown, and China's official stance toward dissidents and ethnic minorities. Each group should then make a short speech about how the international community might respond to such events.

China's Recent History Has Been Full of Turmoil

Judith Banister

The Communist regime that continues to govern China took power in 1949 and called the new state the People's Republic of China (PRC). In the following viewpoint, Judith Banister examines the short history of this regime. Among her focuses is the very fast pace of change in the country since 1949. China's population has continued to expand; its economic transition from agriculture to industry has caused uncertainty, chaos, and tragedy; and the status of ethnic minorities remains a problem. Banister also notes that as the leaders of a one-party authoritarian state, Chinese officials have little tolerance for dissent or opposition. Banister is a recognized expert in global population studies. She is the author of China's Changing Population.

China is a complex civilization with a history spanning several millennia. Since the success of a Communist-led revolution in 1949, China has been known as the People's Republic of China (PRC). For the most part, its borders have been unchanged since then. However, there is some disputed territory

Judith Banister, *Encyclopedia of Modern Asia*. New York: Charles Scribner's Sons, 2002, pp. 503–508. Copyright © 2002 by Global Rights & Permissions, a part of Cengage Learning, Inc. All rights reserved. Adapted from the original and reproduced by permission. www .cengage.com/permissions.

on the high Himalayan borders between Tibet, which is under PRC control, and India. In a remarkably peaceful transition, Hong Kong (a port on China's southern coast) returned to PRC sovereignty from British colonial control in 1997 and nearby Macao from Portuguese colonial control in 1999. The thriving island economy of Taiwan, off the coast of the China mainland, is populated by Chinese people; whether or not it is a part of China is in dispute.

At the start of the twenty-first century, China, with 21 percent of the total global population, is the world's most populous nation. Its vast territory covers an extreme range of altitudes, climates, landforms, and natural resources. The PRC is a poor country that is developing rapidly. Its economy is one of the fastest growing on earth. Its government is one of the world's few remaining Communist regimes. The political system is struggling to remain viable by transforming China from a command economy to a successful socialist market economy. The social transformation of China's people is also breathtaking. To understand what is going on in Asia during the early twenty-first century, it is essential to comprehend the rapid changes taking place in China. . . .

The Political Climate

During the PRC's first twenty-seven years, during which the nation was led by Chairman Mao Zedong (1893–1976), China's totalitarian government established and maintained tight control of the population, right down into families. A U.S.-led embargo isolated China starting in the early 1950s; at the same time, China closed off its borders and defended itself from any perceived colonial or imperialist threats. Especially from the late 1950s through the subsequent decade, China heightened its own isolation, suppressing most information about what was happening in the country and focusing inward. The Communist government attempted to overcome the past and transform the beliefs and ideas of China's people, using a succession of disruptive and even catastrophic ideological movements, including the Great Leap Forward from 1958 to 1961 and the Cultural Revolution of the late 1960s and the 1970s. Arbitrary imprisonment, murder, maiming, and other forms of political harassment and physical harm were commonplace during the Maoist decades.

After Mao's death in 1976, his successors Deng Xiaoping (1904–1997) and then Jiang Zemin (b. 1926) instituted some political changes. As a result, the Communist Party greatly reduced its intrusion into people's personal and family lives. Other improvements include experiments with local village elections and attempts to establish and strengthen a legal system to replace arbitrary rule. But the whole political and economic system is riddled with corruption. Political rights in China are still very limited and human rights are frequently violated. Since troops massacred demonstrators in and around Beijing's Tiananmen Square in 1989, the government has cracked down on democratic movements and unofficial religious groups. Because capitalist and democratic ideas from abroad have eroded the perceived legitimacy of the Communist government in the eyes of the people, the government is now using nationalism to rally its citizens. By Western and advanced Asian standards, the people of China today do not yet have a free press or independent media, freedom of association, freedom of religion, or free speech. . . .

Economic Conditions

In 1949, almost the entire Chinese population was engaged in subsistence agriculture. Only 11 percent of the people lived in urban areas. Modern industry had been brought in by foreign colonial powers only to the coastal city of Shanghai and the northeast provinces (Manchuria). China's Communist government used the Soviet Union as its model of economic development: Starting in the mid-1950s, China's leadership collectivized agricultural land and siphoned off surplus rural production for investment in heavy industry in the cities. This system successfully promoted China's rapid heavy industrialization, but the distortions it introduced into the economy were serious and long-lasting. For example, laborers were prevented from leaving the countryside even if they could be more productive in a town or city. Further, the rural and urban structures of compensation were remarkably flat, and incomes were kept extremely low. The minimal or nonexistent rewards for educational attainment, efficiency, creativity, or work effectiveness in urban and rural areas suppressed incentives to work hard and to excel.

By the 1970s, it was clear to many of China's leaders that certain parts of the economy were not succeeding. Collective agriculture was barely able to keep grain production ahead of China's rapid population growth, and per capita production of other essential foods had declined since the 1950s. In 1978, Deng Xiaoping launched the economic reform period, which began with the abandonment of collectivized agriculture and the return of agricultural land-use rights to each rural family. The government also raised the official purchase prices of grain and other agricultural commodities, and greatly increased the supply of chemical fertilizer. In response, agricultural production increased rapidly in the early 1980s. Simultaneously, the government began to allow rural industries (called "township and village enterprises," or TVEs), light industries, provision of services, village and street markets, and private companies. With this partial introduction of a market economy, growth of the gross domestic product has averaged 8 percent a year since 1978. On the whole, the piecemeal dismantling of China's command economy and gradual introduction of market forces has been a success.

One factor in this success has been the invigoration of rural and urban work incentives in a liberalized policy environment. Another element has been China's opening to the outside world during the economic reform. The booming economy has been based partly on export-led growth, as foreign investors have set up companies and joint ventures in the coastal provinces to make light industrial products for the global market. A third element

The People's Republic of China was led by Mao Zedong during its first twenty-seven years. © AP Images.

has been a belated and ongoing shift of laborers from agriculture to industry and services, accompanied by a policy change allowing some migration out of rural areas for work in towns, cities, and other parts of the country. Surplus rural laborers can now more easily go where their work is in greater demand. . . .

Peoples and Ethnicity

China has a largely homogeneous population based on its officially designated ethnic categories. The Han Chinese nationality comprises 92 percent of the population, though there are some intragroup differences among the category defined as Han Chinese. The fifty-five minority nationalities are unevenly distributed throughout the country. In most of China's populous provinces, only from 1 to 2 percent of the population is non-Han. In general, each minority group is concentrated in one province or several contiguous ones. In only two provinces are Han Chinese in the minority: Tibet in the west and Xinjiang in the northwest. Most of China's land border regions are inhabited by minority nationalities with ethnic kin across the border, which, from the government's perspective, causes major security problems.

Most of China's minority nationalities have been strongly influenced by the Chinese language, historical Chinese culture, and powerful intrusions during the Communist period. Many of the minority groups are highly assimilated. Others remain distinctive in their religion, clothing, housing, language, food, lifestyle, economic life, arts, or customs. Most of the minorities appear to have adapted to overwhelming Han numerical dominance, but some members of certain minority nationalities (Tibetans, along with Uighurs and some other Muslim minorities) are particularly restive. Policies toward the minorities have varied over time. At the beginning of the twenty-first century, some of the minority groups are allowed to have one (or more than one) additional child per couple above the quota for Han Chinese. Other preferential policies are financial subsidies, health and economic assistance, and some affirmative action programs to give the minorities political representation or educational advantages. At the same time, China's government suppresses minority individuals or groups campaigning for freedom of expression and religion, genuine autonomy within the PRC, or independence. . . .

The Social Structure

For a century, the experiences of each new generation in China have differed vastly from the experiences of the previous generation. A series of cataclysmic events—collapse of the last dynasty, civil war, the Japanese invasion, Communist social transformation, attacks on certain social groups, famine, the Cultural Revolution—traumatized tens or hundreds of millions of people at vulnerable stages in their life cycle. At the same time, Chinese society was permanently transformed in many positive ways as well. China's brutal traditional custom of binding and breaking the feet of girls and women completely ceased in the twentieth century, saving hundreds of millions of girls from this crippling disfiguration. The social position of China's girls and women rose sharply in that century, a wrenching cultural shift in any society. There has been vast, generally positive change in male-female relationships. Quality of life for almost all China's people has improved to a stunning degree, especially with regard to survival and health, quantity and variety of food, education, and living standards.

Though China remains primarily rural, the urban proportion of the population increased from 11 percent in 1949 to 36 percent at the end of the twentieth century. Communist policies have set up an economic, political, and social structure that gives extreme advantages to the urban population at the expense of rural people. The World Bank reports that rural incomes are less than one-third of urban incomes, a difference much higher than in most countries. Barriers to geographic and social mobility instituted or strengthened in the Maoist period continue to hold down rural incomes. However, the economic reform period has lifted the great majority of the population out of absolute poverty; remaining pockets of poverty tend to be in mountainous and remote areas.

China in the Twenty-First Century

At the beginning of the twenty-first century, China's people and government wish for the nation to take its rightful place of leadership in global affairs. In many ways, the PRC does function as a responsible, sometimes forward-looking international leading nation. It is an active member of most United Nations organizations, the World Bank system, and many Asian regional organizations. Other Asian nations tend to treat China with caution and respect, in part because of its huge population and territory and rising economic clout, and in part out of fear of possible Chinese aggression. For example, China claims vast reaches of the South China Sea and East China Sea in areas much closer to other countries and claimed by them also. China's unilateral occupation of islands in the disputed regions has raised widespread concern.

Compared with most other developing countries and with other countries in transition from command economies to market or capitalist economies, the PRC is succeeding extraordinarily well. China's biggest economic problem today is employment. The age structure is greatly concentrated in the working-age groups, and the population of working age is still increasing rapidly. As a legacy of China's traditional economy and of Maoist economics, China has one or two hundred million surplus laborers in agriculture, plus tens of millions of surplus workers in industry and government. About one-third of the state-owned enterprises are reported to be losing money, including many of the larger ones. The banking system that has been propping them up is crippled by nonperforming loans to the state sector. Transforming the economy to increase efficiency and productivity means at least temporarily laying off surplus rural and urban workers. The biggest economic challenge is to generate new employment opportunities for those adults who are unemployed, laid off, underemployed, or looking for more productive employment.

China's government is trying to prove that a Communist one-party political system is still viable in the modern world, even though most such governments have now collapsed. The pervasiveness of corruption at all levels weakens the government's claims to popular legitimacy. The government is trying to

confront the corruption problem and shrink the bloated bureaucracy, but the perceived necessity of keeping the Communist
Party in power at all costs continues to mean denying democratic freedom to China's people, imprisoning those who speak
out against autocracy, arresting and suppressing journalists,
preventing people from forming nongovernmental organizations, and biasing the content of education. As China's people
become wealthier, more educated, and in greater contact with
international norms, the PRC political system becomes less viable over time.

Chinese society and culture have been weakened and transformed in myriad ways both by the Communist government
from within and by foreign influences from without. Change
has been so fast and confusing that many Chinese people are
experiencing a spiritual and cultural vacuum. One of China's big
issues in the twenty-first century is to build a modern, stable
society that satisfies the needs of China's own people as they per-
ceive them.

China's historic demographic transition from traditional
high death and birth rates to modern low death and birth rates is
nearly complete. The process occurred very quickly. This implies
that in the coming decades, China will experience rapid and extreme aging of its population structure. Elderly dependency will
place great burdens on China's families and on society because
of the escalating needs of the aged for health care, personal care,
and financial support.

The cumulative harm to China's environment caused by population growth, rising affluence, industrialization, and the low
priority given to addressing this environmental destruction is
another concern. Annual economic losses from pollution, defor-
estation, erosion, desertification, and other ecological disasters
are estimated to equal 5–10 percent of China's gross domestic
product. Many of China's leaders would like to postpone clean-
ing up China's environmental problems until China is a rich
country more easily able to afford the cost, but others argue that

the losses are too massive and the country must reverse the deterioration immediately.

The Future

China has just experienced a century of instability and rapid change in most aspects of life. Almost every part of Chinese society is still in flux. Economic transformation continues unabated. Living standards are rising and lifestyles are changing fast. Politics is shifting more slowly. China may follow the pattern already seen in many other Asian societies, in which economic development has preceded political development, with democratization lagging a decade or two behind the achievement of fairly high incomes and educational attainment. The achievement of full equality between males and females will take decades more. Continuing urbanization will tilt the balance away from conservative rural customs and attitudes. As China continues to modernize, it may come to resemble more closely Taiwan or Hong Kong, places where Chinese culture has adapted to the interconnected global system without losing its distinctive characteristics. Nevertheless China, by virtue of its huge geographic and population size, will remain unique in many respects.

Leader Mao Zedong Discusses the People's Communes of the Great Leap Forward

Mao Zedong

At the time of the Great Leap Forward, Mao Zedong (1893–1976) was the leader of the People's Republic of China. Mao had led the Chinese Communist Party since the 1920s and spearheaded the party's move to power in 1949. In the following viewpoint, taken from a discussion at a meeting of Communist Party officials in 1958, Mao asserts that the Great Leap Forward was a way to strengthen Communist ideology throughout the country. By building on an existing foundation of agricultural producers' cooperatives (APCs), his government would establish people's communes for agricultural and industrial production. There, working together without any need or desire for individual profit, millions of peasants would maintain a revolutionary outlook. Even high officials and military officers, Mao asserts, should be ready for manual labor. This emphasis on ideology as opposed to the proper production and distribution of food likely contributed to the famines of the Great Leap Forward.

Mao Zedong, *The Secret Speeches of Chairman Mao: From the Hundred Flowers to the Great Leap Forward*, edited by Roderick MacFarquhar, Timothy Cheek, and Eugene Wu. Cambridge, MA: The Council on East Asian Studies/Harvard University, 1989, pp. 430–438. Copyright © 1989 by Harvard University Asia Center, the President and Fellows of Harvard College. All rights reserved. Reproduced by permission.

The people's communes have been set up as a result of the masses' initiative; it wasn't us who advocated it. We advocated uninterrupted revolution, eradicating superstition, liberating thought, and daring to think, daring to speak, daring to act; [and] the masses have risen [to the occasion]. [We] did not anticipate this at the Nanning conference, the Chengdu conference, or the second session of the Eighth Party Congress [earlier policy meetings]. The spontaneity of the masses has always been an element inherent in communism. First there was utopian socialism, classical materialism, and dialectics; then came the summation [of these theories] by Marx and others. Our people's communes have been developed on the basis of the APCs [agricultural producers' cooperatives]; they've not come into being from nowhere. We need to understand this clearly in order to systematize this question.

The characteristics of the people's communes are one, big, and two, public. [They have] vast areas of land and abundant resources [as well as] a large population; [they can] combine industry, agriculture, commerce, education, and military affairs, as well as . . . farming, forestry, animal husbandry, sideline production and fisheries—being "big" is terrific. [With] many people, there's lots of power. [We say] public because they contain more socialism than do the APCs, [and they will] gradually eradicate the vestiges of capitalism. For example, the eradication of private plots and private livestock rearing, the running of public mess halls, nurseries, and tailoring groups so that all working women can be liberated. They will implement a wage system and agricultural factories [in which] every single man, woman, old person, and youth receives his own wage, in contrast to the former [system of] distribution to the head of the household. Direct payment of wages is much welcomed by the youth and by women. This eradicates the patriarchal system and the system of bourgeois rights. Another advantage of [cooperatives] being public is that labor efficiency can be raised higher than in APCs.

Communes Will Replace Private Ownership

Currently there are 700,000 APCs nationwide. It would be best to establish big APCs of 10,000 people or 10,000 households. Henan [Province] advocates 2,500 households or so in each; that's all right, too. This is a new problem, but once you disseminate the news, explain the reasons, [then] perhaps in only a few months—through the autumn, winter, and spring—it could be accomplished, more or less. Of course, it will still require a transition period to achieve a wage system and free meals, perhaps a year; for some places perhaps three years. In [our] draft resolution there's a passage [about it taking] one to two or four to five years or even a bit longer to make the transition from the system of collective ownership to the system of communist ownership— almost the same as in the factories—that is, public ownership of all eating, clothing, and housing. The Soviet Union still encourages the construction of houses by private individuals. We will eliminate private housing in the future. . . .

Eliminate Ranks, Bureaucracies, Even Salaries

The first precondition for communism is plenty; the second is to have a communist spirit. Once an order is issued, everyone automatically goes to their work, idlers are few or none. Communism does not differentiate between superiors and subordinates. We have a twenty-two-year history of war communism, with no salaries, [which is] different from the Soviet Union. In the Soviet Union [it's] called the system of surplus grain collection. We didn't practice that. Ours was called the supply system, [in which] army and civilians, officers and men are equal, [and there are also] the three great democracies. Originally we divided up the leftovers from the mess and had small subsidies. After we came into the cities, it was said that the supply system was backward, guerrillaism, a rural work style, [and] that it couldn't boost initiative, nor stimulate progress. [They] wanted to establish a salary system. [They] endured for three years, [and] in 1952 the salary system was established. [They] said bourgeois ranks and rights and such were very fine and called our old supply system a backward method, a guerrilla practice that affected activism. In effect [they] turned the supply system into a system of bourgeois right, [thereby] promoting bourgeois ideology.

Did initiating the 25,000 li [about 8,000 miles] Long March, the Land Revolution and the War of Liberation [earlier Communist transformations] rely on salaries? Two to three million people during the anti-Japanese war [1937–1945], from four to five million during the War of Liberation lived a life of war communism, no Sundays [off]—didn't [they all] risk their lives? The party, the administration, the army, the civilians—numbering several million—all were together with the masses, supporting the administration and loving the people. The party, the administration, and the army under a unified leadership had nothing "to spend," but [with] unity between officers and men, and between the army and civilians, and the support for the administration and love for the people, [we] drove off the Japanese devils and defeated Chiang Kai-shek [opponent during the War of Liberation, 1945–1949]. Nor did [we] have anything "to spend" when we fought the United States. Can it be said [we did all this] because we handed out salaries? Now [we] have something "to spend," issuing salaries according to rank, dividing [them into] generals, field rank officers, and junior officers; but some of them have not even been in battle. Whether or not they're any good has yet to be tested. The result is divorce from the masses; the men don't love their officers, and the masses don't love their cadres [officials]. Because of this we're not much different from the Nationalist party [Chiang Kai-shek's movement]: our garments are in three colors, our food is divided into five grades, even the desks and chairs of our offices are ranked; [and so] the workers and peasants don't like us, saying, "You're officials—party officials, government officials, military officials, commercial officials"—so many officials, how can there be no "isms"? Too many bureaucratic airs, too little politics, so bureaucratism emerges.

Mao Zedong and Maoism

The founder of the People's Republic of China, and its leading figure from the regime's takeover in 1949 until his death in 1976, was Mao Zedong. His ruling philosophy, a version of communism known generally as Maoism, helped to provide the foundation for such events as the Great Leap Forward and the Cultural Revolution. Maoism emphasizes the central role of the masses in staging and winning a violent revolution against imperialist and "bourgeois" (capitalist) forces in society. It also claims that the creation of a Communist society is a long-term effort and not something that can happen immediately after a successful seizure of power. According to Mao, communism requires a high stage of economic development, which China did not have in 1949. It also requires a continual struggle against the bourgeois or reactionary ideas that may remain in place.

Mao was one of the founders of the Communist Party of China (CPC) in 1921, and he rose to leadership during the Long March (1934–1935), when the CPC established a strong base of power in China's rural interior. During World War II (1937–1945 in China), Mao's forces staged a widespread guerrilla war against the Japanese occupiers and, in a civil war that lasted from 1945 to 1949, the CPC defeated the Nationalists who for several decades had

Since the Rectification [Campaign] [1942–1944; an earlier ideological struggle] we have been rectifying bureaucratic airs and putting politics in command. [Since then] the cases of competing for rank and scrambling for special treatment have not been many. I think [we should] get rid of this thing. The salary system does not have to be abolished immediately, because there are professors. But [we should] prepare for it in one or two years. Once the people's communes are established, [this] will force us gradually to abolish the salary system. Since we came into the cities, [we have been] under the influence of the bourgeoisie.

been the internationally recognized leaders of China. As the Nationalists fled to Taiwan, Mao announced the birth of the People's Republic
in October 1949.

Mao's years in control were full of conflict, upheaval, and tragedy—
a reflection, according to Maoists, of the difficulty in establishing a Communist society after a successful revolution. As part of the PRC's early
economic reforms, land was taken away from traditional landlords and
well-off farmers. Many landlords and farmers were beaten and killed, as
were Nationalist officials and sympathizers. Efforts to expand China's
industrial base came before and during the Great Leap Forward (1958–
1962), often with disastrous results. Mao tried to encourage political
diversity with the Hundred Flowers Campaign of 1956, but he ultimately
rejected his own plan and targeted those offering "dangerous" ideas
with imprisonment and execution.

The Cultural Revolution from 1966 to 1976 was the last of Mao's
great legacies. In it, he tried to remind China's masses of the need for
continual revolutionary action to root out old ideas and traditions. During
the Cultural Revolution, Mao became an object of adoration, praised by
groups of youthful Red Guards who carried an edition of Mao's statements known as the Little Red Book. The excesses of the Cultural Revolution ultimately led to the decline in Mao's influence as he aged. After
Mao died in September 1976, a group of hard-line Maoists known as
the Gang of Four tried to seize control, only to be outmaneuvered by
reformers who had different plans for China.

[When] we launched a campaign, it was a really Marxist practice
and a democratic work style, [but] they branded us [as using]
"rural work style" and "guerrilla practices." "Guerrilla practices"
are capitalists' words.

[It was] probably during the period from 1953 to mid 1957
when they did things together with the bourgeoisie, local tyrants,
and evil gentry [that they began to] straighten their clothes, sit
properly, and study the bourgeois style—having haircuts and
shaves, shaving three times a day—all learned from the same
source. . . . What was truly Marxist stuff became unpopular.

Now it's back again: "rural work style" and "guerrilla practice" are Marxist work styles. Thus, speak of equality, the equality between officers and men, and between the army and civilians, and no Sundays [off]; the common people say, "The old Eighth Route [Army] has come back." They are seeing the Eighth Route Army of the past again. . . .

An Industrial Army

In some places the people's communes have adopted a military organization with divisions, regiments, battalions, and companies, and in other places they have not; but "Organize along military lines, work as if fighting a battle, live in a disciplined way," this three-transformations slogan is very good. This is a great industrial army, capable of increasing production, improving life, [and] providing rest; capable of learning; and capable of engaging in military democracy. It seems as soon as [we] talk of the military, we just exclude democracy, but democracy—namely the three great democracies in military affairs, in politics, and in economics—originated precisely in the military. In battle everyone helps each other. [When] officers oppress soldiers in our army, it's a violation of our discipline, it's a disgrace. The "three transformations" in the communes are very good. In the past few years we have learned this stuff, first from the bourgeoisie which is indigenous, second from the proletariat—our Soviet Elder Brother. Luckily, it hasn't been long, so the roots are not deep; revolution is still easy to make.

Since [the 1957] Rectification, various kinds of rules and regulations have almost all been discarded, [and] much of the bourgeois stuff has been jettisoned. This time the army is going to hold a conference to eliminate "spending." We've written a resolution on cadres participating in manual labor: the members of the Center [top leaders] must [do] a month a year; other cadres will [need to do] more, excluding the old and infirm. How can it be as little as a month when you plant an experimental field? A division commander in Yunnan [province] went down to be an [ordinary] soldier in a company. I think many "commanders"—army commanders, division commanders, and so on—all ought to serve as soldiers for at least a month [a year]. In the first year, it'd be best [to do it] for two months. They must obey the commands of squad leaders and platoon leaders. Every year you command the others for eleven months—why can't you let others command you for one month? Some were [ordinary] soldiers once, but have not been for many years. Now they should become soldiers again for a while. Civilian cadres should participate in manual labor for at least one month a year. During the construction of the Ming Tombs Reservoir, even many ministers participated in manual labor. Learn agriculture one year and industry another. Learning them in turn, one is bound to master these two skills. Militarizing the people's communes is not militarization in a bourgeois manner. There is discipline and democracy; the interrelationship is one between colleagues, persuasion rather than coercion. Manual labor needs strict discipline.

As the whole people [begins] to run industry, a certain amount of chaos has temporarily appeared, [because] the boundaries [of authority] are not yet clearly drawn. At this conference, industry, agriculture, commerce, education, and the army have all been topics; but the priority is industry, the whole party and the whole people running industry.

Unintended Famines and Other Catastrophes Resulted from China's Great Leap Forward

R.J. Rummel

In terms of deaths, China's Great Leap Forward is one of the major tragedies of the twentieth century. In the following viewpoint, R.J. Rummel examines the reasons·why millions were victims of the event. Some died from misplaced agricultural policies, which led to famine; ultimately China had to import food to feed its population. Others died during the crushing of rebellions or uprisings. Some were victims of political and ideological crackdowns or died in prisons or forced labor camps. Rummel suggests that more than 40 million people died in just a few years. Rummel is professor emeritus of political science at the University of Hawaii. His books include Death by Government: Genocide and Mass Murder in the 20th Century *and* Power Kills.

The effects of collectivization and the "Great Leap" were disastrous. Already in 1959, the negative effects on public welfare evident in previous years were multiplying. For example, *Honan Peasant's Daily*, a provincial newspaper, disclosed that numerous peasants died from overwork or malnutrition that summer. During two summer weeks, 367,000 collapsed and 29,000 died in the fields. Other papers revealed that over a similar period 7,000 so died in Kiangsi, 8,000 in Kiansu, and 13,000 in Chekiang.

The peasant was trapped by these conditions. Forbidden to leave his commune or work place, only rebellion was left. From 1959 to 1960, at least five of China's provinces saw armed uprisings that could not be suppressed for over a year. . . . In 1959, rebellions took place over a large area in Chinghai, Kansu, and Schechwan; and during the same year Chinese, Hui, and Uighur [the latter two are minority groups] forced laborers rebelled together and destroyed trucks, mines, bridges, and tunnels.

Many Millions Died from Starvation

But all this was part of the build up to the worst famine ever suffered by any country. Consider that from 1877 to 1878 in northern China, an incredible 9,500,000 people starved to death; an equally astounding 7,000,000 in the Soviet Union from 1932 to 1933. But according to the demographer John Aird, an unpublished U.S. Bureau of the Census study, and other informed estimates, during the late 1950s and early 1960s in communist China possibly as many as 40,000,000 died by starvation. In 1960 alone, says PRC economist Sun Zhifang in an official article, the population declined by 11,000,000. Taking into account China's possible population increase, this would mean about 11,000,000 to 30,000,000 deaths in this year alone. However, the demographer Ansley Coale, using official Chinese data and adjusting for underreporting of vital statistics, concluded that 27,000,000 died. Given the many other estimates . . . this seems a most likely figure, as unbelievable as it may be.

This famine . . . was largely the result of failed communist policies and the grandest, most ambitious, most destructive social engineering project ever: the total communization and nationalization of an agriculture system involving over half-a-billion human beings and its reduction to military-like central planning and administration, and the vast and hurried "Great Leap Forward."

Wide-scale drought there was, affecting 41 percent of the farmland in 1959 and 56 percent from 1960 to 1961. This doubtlessly triggered the Great Famine and might have caused a million or so deaths had it occurred in the 1930s. But now the agricultural system was in such disarray and social policies were so counterproductive that the greatest of all famines was inevitable. Consider that beginning in 1950 with "Land Reform" and accelerated after 1955 with the introduction of agricultural cooperatives, the areas subjected to natural calamities increased in direct proportion to the degree of intervention by central party planners. In 1950, 13 million acres of total farmland were hit by natural calamities; 29 million in 1954, 38 million in 1956, 78 million in 1958, 107 million in 1959, and 148 million in 1960.

Bad Policies

With collectivization, peasants—now state workers of public land—understandably had lost their motivation to farm, and, in any case, were bureaucratically organized into inefficient teams and brigades. But aside from this, many party policies directly contributed to worsening the famine. For one there was an inadequate public investment in agriculture compared to industry (16.8 percent of that is industry); for another 90,000,000 peasant workers had been removed from farming to produce the "Great Leap Forward" and another 30,000,000 to work in rural construction programs, sharply cutting into agricultural production.

Production was diminished much further when planners believed their own grossly inflated production statistics. Cadres [officials] down the chain of command would exaggerate agricultural production to meet or surpass already optimistic quotas, and thus creating nationally aggregated figures that far surpassed the actual harvest. But it was on these figures that a fixed tax was calculated, thus taxing away much of the harvest; and it was these figures that made food seem bountiful, thus encouraging planners to reduce the amount of land to be cultivated by 12 percent. . . .

Commune workers build a reservoir to irrigate farmland in 1959, a time when China was experiencing wide-scale drought. © AP Images.

Add to this that the party forcibly purchased excessive amounts of food, leaving too little in reserve for the communes, and that the communes' attempts to adjust to these demands were hampered by the intervention of cadres that knew little about farming or local conditions. Relayed from the central bureaucracy to the different outlying communes came the same commands about how deep to plow, how close to sow, when and what to plant, what seeds to use, how much fertilizer to spread, and what fields to allow to lie fallow. Since these instructions rarely fit local soil and climatic conditions, food production severely suffered.

No wonder that the agricultural system was all but destroyed. And that a probable 27,000,000 human beings starved to death.

These dead, as responsible as party policies were for them, do not in my judgment constitute democide [the murder of people by a government]. It was manslaughter, not murder. These deaths were unintentional, unlike the Ukrainian famine of 1932–33 in the Soviet Union. . . .

Nor could it be said that there was a practical intention here, a wanton disregard for human life that constitutes murder. For unlike the Soviet Union when faced with the Ukrainian famine or the nationalists faced with the Honan famine of 1942 to 1943, as soon the party was convinced that a famine existed, it moved to rectify the underlying social conditions—to restructure the communes and decentralize agricultural policy. For example, among other significant "steps backward," private plots for the peasants were restored.

But food also had to be immediately imported to feed the starving. The policy had been to export food even though the population at best had barely enough to eat. In 1957, for example, China had an export grain surplus of 700 thousand tons. But as the average caloric intake may have dropped to less than 1,500 a day per person (the international standard for a man working a hard eight-hour day is 3,100–3,900 calories) during the famine, it purchased 6,200,000 tons of wheat in 1961, mostly from Australia and Canada. Over the period 1961 to 1965 it imported 29,700,000 tons of grain.

Of course, as in the Soviet Union, those on high who were responsible for all this suffered not at all. . . .

This, added to privation and famine, was enough for some people. As in 1959 and 1960, many continued to resort to armed rebellion. During 1961 and the following year in southern China, there was continuous guerrilla warfare, and Fukien Province, across from Taiwan, also saw a serious armed uprising. A former army officer, a Colonel Chung, led some 8,000 peasants to attack the militia and loot granaries in Wuhua. During 1961 alone, official sources admit that resistance included 146,852 granary raids, 94,532 arsons, and 3,738 revolts. In addition, according to General Hsieh Fu-chih, the Minister of Security, there were 1,235 murders of party and administrative cadres.

Beyond Famine, Millions More Died

Such rebellions and the economic and human costs of collectivization and the "Great Leap" forced the party to reevaluate this jump to communism. Reality had been tested by ideological doctrine, and reality won. The resulting decentralization, deinstitutionalization, and decollectivization that began [were] ultimately to lead to the civil war called the "Cultural Revolution."

The shocking human tragedy of this period, the sheer political drama of the communist social construction and destruction, obscures the continuing party-directed mass movements, such as the "Suppression of the Five Black Categories" ("landlords," "rich peasants," "reactionaries," "bad elements," and "rightists"—considering the previous movements that presumably liquidated these people, one can only wonder at who now was made to fit these black labels) and "Suppressing Anti-Tyranny." There was also the day-by-day sentencing of thousands to forced labor, and the everyday terror. Amazingly, the PRC [People's Republic of China] even fought a short border war with India in 1962 (about 1,000 Chinese were killed in battle), and put down the 1959 revolution in Tibet. . . .

Overall, including forced labor dead and exclusive of the famine and any battle-dead, the democide during these years was 4,244,000 to 21,955,000 killed, probably about 10,729,000. For this one period alone, this is over 1,700,000 more corpses than accumulated in all the battles of World War I, including the famous and gory battles of Verdun, the Marne, and the Somme. And not even included are the 27,000,000 starved to death in the Great Famine.

China's Red Guards Make Their Aims and Tactics Known

Congress of the Red Guards of Universities and Colleges in Peking (Beijing)

A few years after the failures of the Great Leap Forward, which resulted in a lessening of his authority, Mao Zedong tried to reassert his power with the Great Proletarian Cultural Revolution. The Cultural Revolution (1966–1976) was a broad-based attempt to revive revolutionary enthusiasm by overturning traditional social norms. At its heart was a reverence for Mao Zedong Thought, or Maoism, which heavily criticized "reactionaries" who followed the "capitalist road." Many of those deemed to be reactionary were imprisoned, publicly humiliated, or killed.

In the early years of the Cultural Revolution, the most active participants were bands of Red Guards, usually high school or college students. In the following viewpoint, an umbrella organization of Red Guard groups in China's capital, Beijing, states its aims. In addition to their enthusiasm for Mao Zedong Thought, the Red Guards express an unwillingness to tolerate any opposition.

Since their first appearance on the eastern horizon, the Red Guards, a new thing and one of great vitality, have received loving care and tremendous support from Chairman Mao, our

The Chinese Cultural Revolution: Selected Documents, edited and with notes by K.H. Fan. New York: Monthly Review Press, 1968, pp. 191–196.

great teacher, great leader, great supreme commander and great helmsman. Nurtured by Mao Tse-tung's thought, the Red Guards have grown in strength and scope.

The Red Guards are an inevitable outgrowth of the new stage in China's socialist revolution and a great pioneering undertaking in the international Communist movement in the sixties of the twentieth century!

A "Political Shock Force"

Since their birth, the Red Guards have been active on the historic stage of the proletarian revolution as a political shock force, showing a dauntless, revolutionary rebel spirit. Since their birth, the Red Guards, taking the invincible thought of Mao Tse-tung as their weapon and having the powerful support of the workers, peasants, and soldiers, have swept aside ghosts and monsters, battered the bourgeois reactionary line, energetically destroyed the old ideas, culture, customs, and habits of the exploiting classes and vigorously fostered the new ideas, culture, customs, and habits of the proletariat, performing immortal exploits for China's great Proletarian Cultural Revolution. Today, under the great red banner of Mao Tse-tung's thought, we Red Guards from Peking's universities and colleges meet here victoriously to form our own new, revolutionary organization—the Congress of the Red Guards.

Chairman Mao, our most respected and beloved great leader, is our supreme commander.

The Party Central Committee headed by Chairman Mao is our supreme command.

The great invincible thought of Mao Tse-tung is our guiding thought.

Democratic centralism is our organizational principle. We will resolutely exercise extensive democracy under the dictatorship of the proletariat, and institute a system of general elections like that of the Paris Commune [a short-lived uprising in France in 1870].

The main body of the Red Guards should be formed by revolutionary students from families of the working people (workers, peasants, soldiers, revolutionary cadres, and other working people). Students of non-working-people of family origin who have deep feeling for Chairman Mao and a proletarian revolutionary spirit and who have consistently shown a rather good political and ideological stand, can also be enrolled.

We will resolutely implement the class line of the great, glorious and correct Communist Party of China headed by Chairman Mao, draw a distinction between ourselves and our friends and the enemy, firmly rely on the revolutionary Left, win over the middle, unite with the great majority, and thoroughly isolate and strike at the handful of counterrevolutionary revisionists and the most reactionary bourgeois Rightists.

Our battle cry is: "Revolution by proletarian revolutionaries is no crime, to rebel is justified!"

We must always hold aloft the great red banner of Mao Tse-tung's thought and run our organization as a great red school of Mao Tse-tung's thought.

Our congress will unswervingly stand on the proletarian revolutionary line that Chairman Mao represents, thoroughly defeat the bourgeois reactionary line, take the 16-Point Decision of the Central Committee of the Chinese Communist Party concerning the great Proletarian Cultural Revolution as the key, and strive to win victory in fulfilling the great historic task of struggling (against and overthrowing those persons who are in authority and taking the capitalist road), criticizing and repudiating (the reactionary bourgeois academic "authorities" and the ideology of the bourgeoisie and all other exploiting classes), and transforming (education, literature and art and all other parts of the superstructure not in correspondence with the socialist economic base).

Chairman Mao teaches us that the basic question of revolution is political power. "All revolutionary struggles in the world are aimed at seizing political power and consolidating it." From

The Cultural Revolution's strongest supporters were bands of Red Guards. © AP Images.

the very start, the great Proletarian Cultural Revolution has been a struggle to seize power. We stage rebellion in order to seize power: that is, under the dictatorship of the proletariat, to recapture power from the handful of persons in the Party who are in authority and taking the capitalist road, and keep it firmly in the hands of the proletarian revolutionaries.

Destroying the Old, Building the New

Chairman Mao teaches us: "We are not only good at destroying the old world, we are also good at building the new." The Marxist principle of smashing the old state machinery must be carried out in those organizations which have become rotten because a handful of persons in the Party who are in authority and taking the capitalist road entrenched themselves there for a long time. Organs of the dictatorship of the bourgeoisie there must be completely smashed and organs of the dictatorship of the proletariat must be rebuilt there; eclecticism, conciliation, reformism, and peaceful transition must never be practiced. The proletarian revolutionaries must ceaselessly strengthen the dictatorship of the proletariat and establish and consolidate the revolutionary new order in the course of struggle. This is the basic guarantee for carrying the great Proletarian Cultural Revolution through to the end.

Chairman Mao teaches us that we must never forget class struggle. The struggle between seizure of power and counter-seizure of power is at present the focus of the struggle of the two classes and the two roads. Like all reactionaries, the handful of persons in the Party who are in authority and taking the capitalist road will never be reconciled to their own failure. In line with Chairman Mao's teaching we must "cast away illusions, and prepare for struggle."

Chairman Mao teaches us: "In order to attack the forces of the counterrevolution, what the revolutionary forces need today is to organize millions upon millions of the masses and move a mighty revolutionary army into action." In order to develop the struggle to seize power from the handful of persons in the Party who are in authority and taking the capitalist road, the prole-tarian revolutionaries must form a great alliance. We advocate that revolutionaries of all circles first form separate alliances among themselves and then bring about the great unity and al-liance of the proletarian revolutionaries of the capital led by the working class and with the workers, peasants, and soldiers as the main body.

An Army of Millions

Chairman Mao teaches us: "Policy and tactics are the life of the Party." In the struggle to seize power from the handful of persons in the Party who are in authority and taking the capitalist road we must act in accordance with the principles and policies of the Party and unswervingly implement the principle of the "three-in-one" combination. Class analysis must be carried out in regard to persons in authority. We must regard those revolutionary lead-ing cadres who are on the side of Chairman Mao as the treasure of the Party, cherish them, defend them, actively support them and warmly welcome them in fighting shoulder to shoulder with us. We must modestly learn from their experience in struggle and accept their correct leadership which conforms to Mao Tse-tung's thought. We should, with profound class feeling, earnestly criticize and repudiate their shortcomings and mistakes and help them to make amends in line with the principle of "learning from past mistakes to avoid future ones, and curing the sickness to save the patient" which Chairman Mao teaches us. The idea of excluding all, opposing all and overthrowing all is contrary to Marxism-Leninism, Mao Tse-tung's thought.

We, the Red Guards, while seizing power from the handful of persons in the Party who are in authority and taking the capitalist road, must at the same time carry out the struggle of seizing power in our own minds, to seize the power of "self-interest," to rebel against it and to defeat it! . . .

To defeat "self-interest," it is necessary to follow the teachings of Chairman Mao, to integrate ourselves with the workers and peasants and, in the course of the three great revolutionary movements (class struggle, the struggle for production, and scientific experiment), thoroughly to remold our world outlook and foster the concept of wholeheartedly serving the workers, peasants, and soldiers. . . .

We, the Red Guards, pledge to be thoroughgoing proletarian revolutionaries. We will always hold high the great revolutionary banner of criticism, be always full of the youth and vitality of revolutionary rebels. Whoever dares to oppose Chairman Mao, to oppose Mao Tse-tung's thought, and foster revisionism in China, no matter how high his position, how senior his service, and how great his renown, we will resolutely rebel against him, and we will rebel to the end! We must always keep New China bright red and smash the dream of the imperialists and modern revisionists to bring about a "peaceful evolution."

We, the Red Guards, will always be vanguard fighters against imperialism and revisionism. We will give all-out support to the struggle of the oppressed people and nations for liberation, firmly stand with them, and thoroughly bury imperialism, revisionism, and all reactionaries in order to carry the world revolution through to the end!

We firmly believe that Communism will triumph! Monsters of all kinds shall be destroyed. The globe in the future will be a world with red flags, will be a world shining with the great thought of Mao Tse-tung!

China's Ethnic Minorities Suffered Greatly During the Cultural Revolution

Colin Mackerras

The Cultural Revolution demanded complete conformity and left little room, as Colin Mackerras writes in the following viewpoint, for China's ethnic minority groups. Although the official policy of the People's Republic of China before and after the Cultural Revolution included the acceptance of minority groups and their customs, the ten years of the Revolution (1966–1976) were marked by attacks on these groups. Mackerras writes of violence directed at Hui Muslims and Tibetans, among others, and notes that even traditional minority-group literature became a target. Colin Mackerras is professor emeritus at Griffith University at Brisbane in Australia. Among his many books are China's Minorities: Integration and Modernization in the 20th Century *and* China in Transformation: 1900–1949.

Although the early 1960s saw a relaxation of policy towards the minorities, this was but a prelude to a period most commentators and minorities have seen as the most repressive and destructive in the PRC [People's Republic of China], namely the Cultural Revolution, lasting from 1966 to 1976. In the latter year

Colin Mackerras, "Historical Background," *China's Ethnic Minorities and Globalization*. New York: Routledge Curzon, 2003, pp. 23–25. Copyright © 2003 by Taylor & Francis Group. All rights reserved. Reproduced by permission of Taylor & Francis Books UK.

Buildings have been reconstructed among the ruins of Ganden Monastery, a casualty of religious persecution during the Cultural Revolution. © Galen Rowell/Corbis.

Mao Zedong, the architect of the Cultural Revolution, died on 9 September and within a month his main supporters had been overthrown and his political legacy was on the way out.

The most important feature of the Cultural Revolution was an ideological narrowness of almost unbelievable dimensions. Only Mao Zedong's thought was allowed currency, and his works were the almost exclusive reading diet of the Chinese people from August 1966 until the end of the 1960s. On 25 December 1967, China's official New China News Agency (NCNA) reported that the number of published copies of *Quotations from Chairman Mao Zedong*, which contained the gems of Mao's sayings, had reached no less than 350 million.

Class Struggle Overshadowed Ethnic Struggle

For ethnic affairs, a particularly vicious part of the ideology of the Cultural Revolution was the obsession with class struggle, which was dubbed 'the key link' on which all else depended. The

CHINA'S ETHNIC GROUPS

KAZAKH

UIGHUR

HUI

TUJIA

TIBETAN

DONG

BAI

YI

HANI

MIAO

ZHUANG

Source: Adapted from Yi Zhou and Matthew Bloch/*The New York Times*, "2000 China Census," China Data Center at the University of Michigan, December 14, 2011. www.nytimes.com.

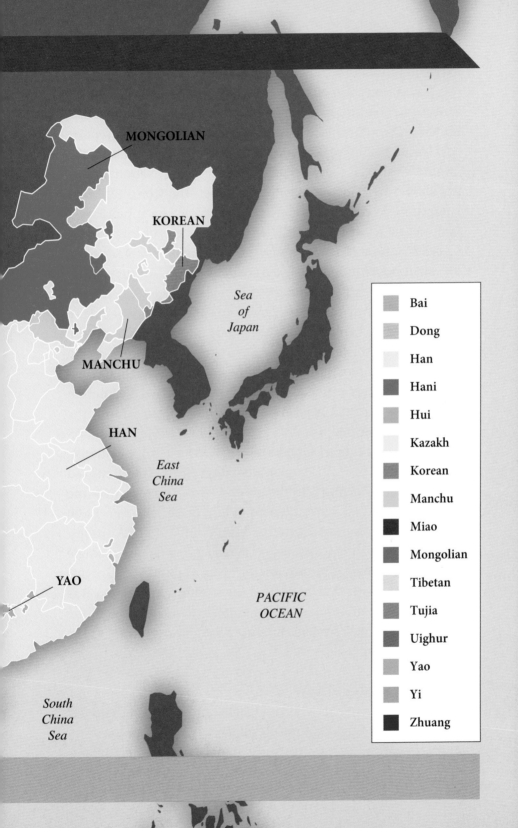

MONGOLIAN

KOREAN

MANCHU

HAN

YAO

Sea
of
Japan

East
China
Sea

PACIFIC
OCEAN

South
China
Sea

	Bai
	Dong
	Han
	Hani
	Hui
	Kazakh
	Korean
	Manchu
	Miao
	Mongolian
	Tibetan
	Tujia
	Uighur
	Yao
	Yi
	Zhuang

implication was that ethnic struggle simply did not matter and was only a reflection of class struggle anyway. It was during the Cultural Revolution that Jiang Qing (1914–1991), Mao's wife and leader of the radical faction known as the 'gang of four', reportedly asked her infamous question, 'Why do we need national minorities anyway?', answering by stating flatly: 'National identity should be done away with!' Although the Constitution of January 1975 retained the concept of autonomy for minorities, a far lower status was accorded it, and in practice it meant nothing.

The Cultural Revolution saw severe instability in many parts of China and periods of localised civil war, such as in Hubei province in August and September 1967. A case of full-scale, though brief, rebellion in the ethnic areas was the Shadian Incident. Following years of repression during the Cultural Revolution, the Hui (Chinese Muslims) of Shadian, a village in Mengzi County of southern Yunnan Province near the border with Vietnam, had wished to reopen a mosque closed due to Cultural Revolution persecution, but had been refused permission. As a result the local Hui established a militia group, leading authorities to accuse them of trying to found an independent Islamic republic. Late in July 1975, PLA [People's Liberation Army] troops moved into the village, razing it to the ground. Fierce fighting over the next week in Shadian and surrounding areas left over 1,600 Chinese Muslims dead, as well as several hundred PLA troops. In terms of casualties, this was certainly among the worst single incidents involving minorities in the history of the PRC. Not until February 1979, by which time the Cultural Revolution was over, were reparations and apologies made to the relatives of the dead, with the government building seven new mosques in the Shadian area.

Forms of Persecution

The Shadian Incident is a good illustration showing two related features of the Cultural Revolution: religious persecution and cultural destruction. In most minority areas religion was banned, with clerics being forced to return to lay life, harmed or even killed, and religious buildings closed, damaged or destroyed. With many minorities, religion and culture are tightly linked. For instance, Tibetan Buddhist monasteries are also major repositories of Tibetan traditional arts, paintings, masks for dancing, and religious statues. Many were damaged and some destroyed. The great Ganden Monastery outside Lhasa [Tibet's capital] sustained damage that has to be seen to be believed. My visit to the great Muli Monastery in western Sichuan Province at the beginning of 1997 revealed ruined buildings alongside the restored ones. In addition, the traditional dramas of the Tibetans, Miao, Koreans, Dong and others were banned, as were their classical literature and poetry, with many books damaged or destroyed. It is not surprising that minorities look back on the Cultural Revolution as a nightmare. Moreover, it is hardly a consolation to know that the Han [majority Chinese] also suffered similar cultural destruction and religious persecution.

A Description of the Government Crackdown in Tiananmen Square

Amnesty International

In the mid-1980s, as Communist China began to open up its economy, university students and a few dissidents began to work for political reforms to accompany the economic progress. By 1989 the pro-democracy movement in China was widespread and vocal. After a pro-reform official, Hu Yaobang, died on April 15, 1989, tens of thousands of protesters began to gather in Beijing's Tiananmen Square demanding political change. The government, fearful of disorder, declared martial law in late May. Then, when protesters refused to leave the square, leaders made the fateful decision to use the People's Liberation Army to stop the protests. Various accounts suggest that many people were killed or wounded. The following viewpoint by international human rights organization Amnesty International pieces together the events in the square the night of June 4, 1989.

Tiananmen is a very large square edged by long buildings on two sides: the Great Hall of the People on the west; the Museum of the Chinese Revolution and the Museum of Chinese History on the east. In the north, Chang'an Avenue separates the

"Our Hearts Were Breaking," *Death in Beijing (Contemporary Report 1989)*. London: Amnesty International British Section, 1989, pp. 25–33. Copyright © Amnesty International UK Section. All rights reserved. Adapted and reproduced by permission.

Square from Tiananmen Gate—the entrance to the Forbidden City. Opposite Tiananmen Gate, on the northern end of the Square, was a statue to the "Goddess of Democracy" erected by students on 30 May [1989]. The Statue was pulled down by troops at around 0500 hours on 4 June. In the southern part of the Square is Chairman Mao's Memorial Hall (referred to hereafter as the Mausoleum) and north of it is the Monument to the People's Heroes—a large column erected on a stepped platform around which Beijing students had established their headquarters. In the south, Qianmen Avenue marks the end of the Square and a large gate—Qianmen Gate—faces it at the crossroad between Qianmen Avenue (east—west) and Qianmen Street (north—south).

The eye-witness statements received by Amnesty International indicate that most civilians killed or wounded in that area were shot on the edges of the Square, particularly in its northern part, as well as in the neighbouring streets.

Official Statements Are Incomplete and Inconsistent[*]

Several public statements made by Chinese officials since 4 June have denied that anyone died during the "clearing" of the Square. These statements, however, refer only specifically to the period of time between 0430 hours and 0530 hours of 4 June, and to the evacuation of the centre south of the Square by students—in other words, they do not refer to what happened before 0430 hours (described below) or to what happened on the edges of the Square. One of the earliest official statements, made by the Propaganda Department of Beijing Municipal CCP [Chinese Communist Party] Committee on 5 June, while denying that many killings had occurred in the Square, said: "As there were many onlookers and students at the Square, some were run down

---

[*] Subheadings were not in the original text but were added by the editors of this volume of Genocide and Persecution.

by vehicles, some were trampled by the crowd, and others were hit by stray bullets". This specific reference to people killed or injured "at the Square" has not been repeated in subsequent official statements. The 5 June statement by the Beijing CCP Committee also narrowed down the time during which "no one was killed" to "less than 30 minutes" between 0500 hours and 0530 hours. It said:

> At around 0500 hours, holding their banners, they [the students] began to move out of the Square in an orderly way. At that time there was still a small number of students who persistently refused to leave. In accordance with the demands of the 'circular' [by the Martial Law command], soldiers of the armed police force forced them to leave the Square. The Square evacuation was completely carried out by 0530 hours. During the entire course of evacuation, which took less than 30 minutes, not a single one of the sit-in students in the Square, including those who were forced to leave the Square at the end, died.

Various sources estimate that the number of people in the Square between midnight and 0300 hours was anything between 30,000 and 50,000. The numbers gradually decreased later. There were also large crowds along East Chang'an Avenue, close to the Square.

Violence and Chaos Begin Overnight*

Some 15 or 20 minutes after midnight on 4 June, two armoured personnel carriers (APCs) came from the south into Tiananmen Square and drove along its sides at high speed. One turned left into West Chang'an Avenue and went all the way up to Xidan. The other one turned right into East Chang'an Avenue. The APC in East Chang'an Avenue was seen by many people driving at a speed estimated by eye-witnesses of 100 kilometres per hour.

---

* Subheadings were not in the original text but were added by the editors of this volume of Genocide and Persecution.

It smashed through barricades along the way, killing and injuring many people. After it passed the Jianguomen intersection, it turned around at the next crossroad and came back again at high speed towards the west. At the Jianguomen intersection, thousands of civilians had blocked a large convoy of trucks full of soldiers for several hours before the APC arrived. The civilians had also dragged a truck filled with soldiers into the middle of the barricades in the road. The APC, on its return journey, came smashing through the crowd and into the truck, overturning it and other vehicles. Several people were killed—including at least one soldier—and several others injured. On its way, somewhere along Jianguomen Avenue, the APC had also reportedly crushed a man on a bicycle. Either the same APC or another one (according to some sources, there were two) was seen again, shortly afterwards, colliding with a truck, driving at full speed from the west towards Tiananmen Square. It went through East Chang'an Avenue. People in the dense crowds present in that area then blocked the APC when it reached Tiananmen Square at around 0100 hours. It was set alight and when soldiers emerged from the burning vehicle the first one was surrounded by people, badly beaten and apparently killed. The others, however, were rescued by students and taken onto a bus. Nevertheless, this incident was later shown on Chinese Central Television as an example of the "counter-revolutionary rebellion" and of "hoodlums on the rampage".

At around 0100 hours in the north of the Square, shooting was heard coming from the west and several big fires could be seen in West Chang'an Avenue. At about 0130 hours, the first trucks full of troops coming from West Chang'an reached the northwest of the Square. At around that time an eye-witness saw five or six people injured at a medical point at the northwest corner of the Square. He assumed that they had been brought into the Square from West Chang'an Avenue by people retreating in front of the troops. As the troops approached and stopped at the corner of West Chang'an, there was a great deal of firing, but most eye-witnesses thought at that stage the troops were either firing into the air or firing blanks or rubber bullets, as they saw few casualties. One journalist described the first two casualties he saw as follows: "a girl with her face smashed and bloody, carried spread-eagled towards the trees. Another followed—a youth with a bloody mess around his chest".

According to two eye-witnesses, after the troops arrived they divided into two groups—one which moved slightly towards the Square and started firing in that direction, and another one which started moving towards Tiananmen Gate but was apparently distracted by a fire in the northwest corner. Several fires were burning in the north of the Square. One of these was the tent of the Independent Federation of Workers (formed during the protests), and bushes were also burning at the northwest corner. The APC which had been stopped earlier by the crowd was also burning further to the east. At that time, a group of about 15 armed police came from the entrance to the Forbidden City (Tiananmen Gate) charging people with batons. Some youths attempted to throw petrol bombs at them. The police charged again, some firing was heard and people ran in panic towards East Chang'an.

Battles in the Square*

Sometime after 0200 hours, a group of soldiers formed in lines across Chang'an Avenue at the level of Tiananmen Gate, facing east. One eye-witness described them as being formed in three lines—one kneeling or crouching, the second one slightly above and the third one standing at the back. They started firing towards the crowds in the northeast of the Square for a few minutes, then stopped. There were at least two more bursts of firing as the soldiers advanced in stages towards East Chang'an Avenue during the next hour or so. Some eye-witnesses said that

---

* Subheadings were not in the original text but were added by the editors of this volume of *Genocide and Persecution.*

firing was also coming from other directions in between volleys of firing from these troops. Some bullets were flying overhead, some ricocheting, some hitting people. The crowds at the corner of East Chang'an were running away during the shooting, then coming back towards the Square in between bursts of firing. Some were singing the Internationale [a widely sung anthem], others shouting slogans. One or two people at the front of the crowd were throwing objects at the troops. Between 0230 hours and 0300 hours, a bus came from East Chang'an Avenue, passed the crowd and drove towards the troops in the northeast corner of the Square. There was some shooting. The bus slowed and stopped. Soldiers surrounded it, smashed the windows and—it is presumed—killed the driver.

The troops reached the northeast corner of the Square at about 0300 hours, sealing the entrance to the Square. They were now in complete control of the north end of the Square. Several sources estimate that by that time around 20 to 30 people had been wounded and "a few" killed by gunfire in that part of the Square. The wounded were carried away by pedicabs.

At 0330 hours, the crowds of civilians in East Chang'an Avenue were gathered near Nanchizi Street. There was a long period of quiet (at least 20 minutes). People in the crowd were relaxing, thinking there would be no more shooting as the troops were now blocking access to the Square. Suddenly, without warning or provocation, the troops started firing again. Several eyewitnesses said there was a lot of firing, louder than previously. They described it as machine-gun fire which lasted for a very long time. One source said that when the firing started the crowds ran away one full block to Nanheyuan, while troops continued to fire at their backs. Some bullets were going over heads. Some people crouched on the ground, others ran into side streets. Several eyewitnesses said they saw many casualties. One source counted between 36 and 38 wounded people being carried away. Some had stomach wounds, others back wounds or leg injuries. Another source, who was at the corner of Wangfujing Street (further east

Several bodies of civilians lie dead near Tiananmen Square after the government crackdown on protesters on June 4, 1989. © AP Images.

in the Avenue), saw many injured people carried away in pedicabs or rickshaws: one man had the top of his head blown away; some had bad chest or stomach wounds.

Student Demonstrators Wait and Prepare*

Meanwhile, in the Square, it was very quiet around the Monument to the People's Heroes. The students' loudspeakers had called on people several times to gather around the Monument. Many were sitting on the steps or around it—some sleeping. Various sources estimated that between 3,000 and 5,000 students were gathered there at around 0330 hours. The atmosphere was calm. A few young workers of the "Dare-to-die" brigades (about two dozen according to one source), had dashed back and forth between the Monument and the north end of the Square earlier. They had stakes and pikes and were determined to sacrifice their

---

* Subheadings were not in the original text but were added by the editors of this volume of Genocide and Persecution.

lives. When troops started coming into the north end of the Square from West Chang'an Avenue, one of them said "I have just smoked my last cigarette". He then dashed off towards the north with others and was never seen again.

By 0330 hours the army was in complete control of the Square. Troops at the north had sealed the entrances to the Square. They had been followed by tanks and APCs which lined up in the north of the Square and stayed there until about 0500 hours. To the east of the Square, a large number of soldiers were sitting in front of the History Museum. To the west, troops were occupying the Great Hall of the People. In the south, troops had arrived at around midnight from West Qianmen Avenue and had taken position in the southwest corner. Other troops later came from the south, firing into the air. According to two eye-witnesses, there was some firing in the south of the Square at around midnight. One said he saw three people, including an old man and an old woman, killed by gunfire when soldiers came from Qianmen Street.

By 0330 hours, in addition to the students around the Monument, there were still many civilians in various places in the Square, particularly along the edges and in the southern part.

A Negotiated Withdrawal*

At 0400 hours, the lights in the Square were suddenly switched off. They came on again about 45 minutes later. (This timing—given by private sources—does not correspond to that given in an official account of events around the Monument, which was published in the *People's Daily* on 24 July 1989. According to the *People's Daily*, the lights were switched off just after 0425 hours and were switched on again at 0530 hours. This official account says that, as the lights were switched off, onlookers in the Square started to disperse, and students closed ranks around

---

* Subheadings were not in the original text but were added by the editors of this volume of *Genocide and Persecution*.

the Monument.) While the lights were off, a quick succession of events occurred in various parts of the Square. A bus came from the southeast corner of the Square and parked near the Monument. It was still calm around there. Then, hundreds of armed soldiers started coming out of the Great Hall of the People. Others moved up from the southwest corner. An APC came rushing from the southeast corner, smashing the barricades along the road that marks the southeast end of the Square. At the Monument, one of four Chinese intellectuals who had been on hunger-strike in the Square since 2 June suddenly announced that they had reached an agreement with the soldiers for students to evacuate the Square through the southeast corner. On their own initiative, the hunger-strikers had negotiated a retreat for the students with the army during the previous hour. Many students and workers did not want to leave; there were speeches and discussions, then a vote. The shouts of those wishing to stay were apparently louder, but a student leader announced that the evacuation had been decided. Groups of students started to leave before the lights came back on and, according to some sources, most had walked away from the Monument by 0500 hours.

Meanwhile, however, a detachment of 200 soldiers among those which had come out of the Great Hall of the People had launched an attack on the Monument, smashing the students' equipment and reportedly beating people in the way with batons. (This assault is described in detail in the *People's Daily* article of 24 July, which also confirms most of the following description.) For a while there was chaos for a while around the Monument and some soldiers started firing. According to some sources (including the *People's Daily* account), the soldiers were firing over people's heads, at the Monument, destroying the students' loudspeakers, and no one was killed. According to other sources, some people at the Monument were hit by bullets. Among others who claim that people were killed at that stage, one Chinese student was cited in press reports on 5 June as saying: "I was sitting down. A bullet parted my hair. Students fell down around me, about 20 to 30. A group of workers protecting us was all killed". Some foreigners, however, say they saw no deaths around the Monument.

At around 0500 hours the tanks and APCs at the north of the Square started driving slowly towards the south, followed by infantry several rows deep. As the troops advanced, the statue of the Goddess of Democracy in the north of the Square was pulled down. Some tents near the statue and further south were crushed by tanks. A large group of students was by then leaving towards the southeast. The tanks slowly came closer to them. The students were slowly walking away with their banners, forming lines linking hands, stopping, and then advancing again. Several foreign journalists have told Amnesty International that they saw the bulk of the student group leave the Square unhurt. However, soldiers were firing towards people along the sides by the time the first tanks and APCs reached the southern end of the Square. By 0600 hours the Square was completely sealed off by troops and army vehicles.

Uncertainty and Mixed Reports*

It is not clear whether some students or other people stayed behind. Government reports say that some people who did not want to leave were "forced" to leave. According to one source, some 200 students stayed in the Square and about 50 of them, badly beaten up, were later reportedly taken by police to a hospital where they were treated for an hour before being taken away by police. Other sources claim that students and other people who stayed behind were shot. It is not clear whether or not this refers to shooting in the southern end of the Square. When some APCs reached the southeast corner and parked along the side road there at around 0530 hours, some eye-witnesses heard a lot of sustained gunfire coming from within the Square. By that time the troops who had come down behind the tanks and APCs were firing in the direction of onlookers gathered on the edges

---

* Subheadings were not in the original text but were added by the editors of this volume of Genocide and Persecution.

of the Square—apparently above their heads in some cases, but people among the groups of onlookers were hit by bullets. One eye-witness in a lane on the southeast side of the Square saw two or three bicycles carrying wounded people, and was told later that people in buildings in the lane had been killed by bullets. A member of the Hong Kong Student Federation saw a student from Beijing Normal University beside him "filled with blood all over his head which nearly exploded"; he died immediately. (*Hong Kong Standard*, 5 June 1989.) A Polish state television reporter said that a student standing one metre from him was shot dead after shouting insults at advancing soldiers; he added that he saw soldiers shooting fleeing students in the back, unprovoked and at random. Another source told Amnesty International that a friend of his was shot in the back of the head at about 0600 hours in the southeast corner of the Square and that the bullet came out by his mouth. The extent of the casualties in the south of the Square, however, is not known.

It is also unclear whether people in tents were crushed by tanks. Between 0300 and 0330 hours, several foreigners checked tents near the statue of the "Goddess of Democracy" in the north of the Square, and some of the tents on the east of the Monument. They found three to five students sleeping in the tents in the north, and "a few" people in those to the east of the Monument. At around 0500 hours two foreigners checked some tents around the Monument and found them empty. The official *People's Daily* account of 24 July says that soldiers who had launched the assault on the Monument checked "every tent with flashlights" and forcibly drove away some "stubborn people" who still refused to leave.

Attacks Outside the Square*

Two other incidents during which students were killed or wounded after they left the Square have been reported. These in-

---

* Subheadings were not in the original text but were added by the editors of this volume of *Genocide and Persecution.*

cidents happened around Liubukou [Street]. Most of the students who left the Square went west into Qianmen Avenue, then headed north into a smaller street, reaching West Chang'an Avenue at Liubukou. When they left Qianmen Gate (south of the Square), the students (numbering several thousands) formed a long column, marching very slowly. It took over an hour for the head of the column to reach Liubukou. There, they turned left into Chang'an Avenue and walked towards the west at around 0600 hours. At that point, several APCs driving at high speed towards the west came from Tiananmen Square and crushed several students, killing 11 people. (A photograph of some of the crushed bodies has been published in various newspapers and magazines.) According to some sources, the APCs were not firing before they crushed the students and one of the APCs stopped while another one went around the scene. Soldiers in a third and fourth APC then reportedly opened fire and threw tear-gas towards the crowd gathered there. The APCs later continued towards the west at high speed. The students were able to collect the bodies of the dead.

One eye-witness, who described the APCs as tanks, has given the following account of the scene:

About six in the morning, it was already light. I was on my bike, and walking with me were some students who had retreated from Tiananmen and were returning to their schools.

As we arrived at Chang'an Street, I saw four tanks coming from the square going west at very high speed. The two tanks in front were chasing students. They ran over the students. Everyone was screaming. We were too. I counted 11 bodies.

The soldiers in the third tank threw tear-gas toward us. Some citizens decided to recover the students' bodies. The fourth tank fired at us with machine-guns. They hit four or five people. After the tanks had passed, some people collected the bodies. I saw two bodies very close: one boy student and one girl. I got a good look. They were flat. Their bodies were all bloody. Their mouths were pressed into long shapes. Their eyes were flat and big. We cried because our hearts were breaking.

Muslim Uighurs in China's Xinjiang Province Face Many Forms of Discrimination

Ross Terrill

In the following viewpoint excerpt, Ross Terrill examines the history of China's largest minority group, the Uighurs. The Uighurs are a people who speak a language related to Turkish and largely practice Islam. Their traditional homeland is Xinjiang, a province in the dry western region of modern China—the People's Republic of China, or PRC. Although modern Chinese leaders claim that Xinjiang has been part of China since the Han Dynasty (204 BC– 220 AD), the truth is more complicated, Terrill maintains. While the Uighurs had a great deal of political independence for many centuries, in recent years they have faced a growing presence of Han, or mainstream Chinese people, in Xinjiang as well as subtle attacks on their culture. Terrill is the author of various books on China including China in Our Time: The Epic Saga of the People's Republic from the Communist Victory to Tiananmen Square and Beyond *and* Flowers on an Iron Tree: Five Cities of China. *He has taught at Harvard University, the University of Texas at Austin, and Monash University in Australia.*

Ross Terrill, Excerpted from "Chapter 9: The Steppe Empire," *The New Chinese Empire.* New York: Basic Books, 2003, pp. 232–236. Copyright © 2004 Ross Terrill. All rights reserved. Reprinted by permission of Basic Books, a member of the Perseus Book Group via Copyright Clearance Center.

Xinjiang takes up one-sixth of the PRC map. It borders eight nations, and is larger than all of Britain, France, Spain, and Italy. In this land rich in oil, tin, mercury, copper, iron, uranium, and lead, four cultural worlds abut: Han, Mongol, Turkic, and Tibetan. One example of the entanglement is Lamaist Buddhism in Tibet and Mongolia, to either side of Xinjiang; the "Dalai" in Dalai Lama is a Mongol word, and the 4th Dalai Lama was a Mongol.

Starting in the fourteenth century, after the fall of the Mongol (Yuan) Dynasty, Islam made huge strides in Xinjiang. Although Buddhism and other faiths remained, by the seventeenth century the area was thoroughly Islamicized.[9] Like Christianity and Judaism, Islam "sprang from a culture that attempted to coordinate the two societies of pastoralism and the oasis and to create a community of outlook in town and tent and field, between trader and peasant and herdsman."[10] That was China's problem with it. Islam became rooted in the desert-plus-oases of Xinjiang because it offered a social sinew that Confucianism could not match.

Most of the Turkic people in Xinjiang are Uighur. Now numbering nine million, the Uighurs became prominent in the region in the seventh century. In 744 they took Mongolia. Later they retreated to their present habitat, leading a partly nomadic life, but practicing some agriculture. A people of notable musical and literary flair, they are nonfanatical Muslims of the Sunni persuasion.

People in Beijing and Shanghai routinely remark, and Chinese children learn in school, that Xinjiang has been China's since the Han. The truth is different. For a thousand years from the eighth century, China-based polities exercised some influence, but no control over the Xinjiang area as a whole. It was the Qing Dynasty that staked out "East Turkistan" for China, and Stalin who

---

[9] James Millward, communication to the author, Oct. 11, 2002.
[10] Lattimore, 1962, 80–81.

China and Tibet

Tibetans are one of the largest of China's ethnic minority groups. Indeed, for much of its history Tibet was effectively an independent state and the Tibetans a free people. Only in 1950—following a short and successful war—did China incorporate Tibet into the People's Republic. Lying in China's far west, the former kingdom is now known as the Tibet Autonomous Region, or Xizang.

The relationship between Tibetans and the Chinese government has been filled with conflict since the takeover. Initially, Tibetan and Chinese officials reached an agreement that would allow the area to maintain a large degree of self-governance under the Tibetan Buddhist leader, the Dalai Lama. Despite this agreement, China soon took steps to install a Communist bureaucracy there. After 1955, rebellions among the Tibetans spread quickly until, in 1959, the Dalai Lama fled to exile in India. By 1965 Tibet was administered simply as a province of the People's Republic.

secured it for Mao's China. In the Muslim view, the Chinese are interlopers. To name the area Xinjiang, "New Border," as the Qing did, was an insult to Uighurs long resident in the Tarim Basin and Turfan area. Of course, the Qing's choice of "New Border" also showed Xinjiang had *not* been China's since the Han Dynasty.

People in eastern China have little idea how colonial is the atmosphere in Xinjiang (and Tibet). Mao called the Soviet Union's presence in Xinjiang in the 1930s "colonialism." Was it so different from the PRC grip? Selective memory stores up danger, just like the fictions of dynasties that declared Barbarians "obedient" when they were hostile (discussed in Chapter 3).

The modern history of Xinjiang and its environs recalls Julian Huxley's remark: "A 'nation' is a society united by a common error as to its origin and a common aversion to its neigh-

The upheaval in Tibet coincided with China's Great Leap Forward. Tibet suffered greatly from the government's heavy-handed attempts at agricultural reforms, as did much of the rest of the country. During the Cultural Revolution, from 1966 to 1976, China destroyed hundreds of Tibetan Buddhist temples and allegedly killed thousands of monks. Chinese leaders also tried to restrict the use of the Tibetan language and, in a process that continues, to replace Tibetan officials with Chinese.

In recent years, China has tried to extend economic development to Tibet. A recently completed railway line connecting its capital, Lhasa, with other Chinese cities is the great symbol of these efforts. In addition, the government has tried to encourage mainstream Han Chinese to migrate to Tibet to live and work. These efforts have inspired continued resistance, even large-scale riots and demonstrations as recently as 2008. Meanwhile, the Tibetan Government in Exile established by the Dalai Lama in Dharamsala, India in 1959 keeps alive a vibrant culture and continues to advocate for greater freedom in Tibet.

bors." In the nineteenth century, Russia and Britain each tried to influence politics in Xinjiang. In the early twentieth century, Turkey backed pan-Turkism in the area. Most dramatically, in the 1940s the Soviet Union encouraged Muslims in the Ili region of northwestern Xinjiang to declare independence from (Chiang Kai-shek's) China.

Across the border, Stalin mixed and matched "republics" in Central Asia, by the 1920s part of the Soviet Union, like a child with a cutout book. He evidently believed that to multiply Turkic identities, including Kazak, Kirghiz, and Uighur, then shuffle them to ensure irrational borders, would forestall pan-Turkism. A Xinjiang warlord of the 1930s, and later Mao as well, learned "minority policy" from Stalin, and rearranged the non-Han peoples in western China to minimize separatism.

As Xinjiang in the nineteenth century was "the most rebellious territory in the Qing empire,"[11] so today, resistance to Beijing's policies in Xinjiang, mainly by Uighurs, is constant. The East Turkistan People's Party, a pro-independence group based outside China, claims to have 60,000 members and 178 underground branches inside Xinjiang.[12]

Doak Barnett wrote that Xinjiang "was, historically, more associated with Central Asia than with China."[13] This is China's Xinjiang problem. During the 1990s, the Taliban regime in Kabul trained a number of militant Muslims from Xinjiang, whose aim is to eject China from Xinjiang and restore the independent state of East Turkistan, which existed as recently as 1945. "The situation in Xinjiang is the main element in China's Afghanistan policy," a Chinese Central Asia specialist said in October 2001.[14] Beijing's efforts with carrot and stick to dissuade the Taliban from meddling in Xinjiang had not solved all problems. By the time 9/11 arrived, the PRC had good reason to wish the Taliban into the trash can of history. That is why Jiang Zemin spoke up for Bush's drive against terrorism.

In Xinjiang, we see apartheid with Chinese characteristics. Towns and streets all have Chinese names, unreadable for most Uighurs. The Han wear the uniforms. All college textbooks are in Chinese. Han regulations strangle the life of the mosques; the Muslim doctrine, "pure and true," is often a cry in the wilderness. Han officials pay Chinese females money if they marry a Uighur—not an everyday occurrence—thus contributing to the melting away of Uighur identity. No one from Xinjiang is permitted to study in Iran or Pakistan. "The Uighur people have suffered for years under Chinese discrimination and oppression," said Abdulhekim, executive chairman of the East Turkistan

---

[11] Fletcher, 1978, 90.
[12] *Taipei Times*, Oct. 11, 1999.
[13] Barnett, 1993, 343.
[14] *Far Eastern Economic Review*, Oct. 4, 2001.

Uighur Muslims, China's largest minority group, pray in the Idkah Mosque in the province of Xinjiang. © Carlos Spottorno/Edit by Getty Images.

Center in Istanbul. "The ethnic hatred is like water boiled to 100 degrees and could explode at any moment."[15]

Hundreds of "splittists" are arrested in a typical month. A sizeable batch of these militant Muslims is executed every few months.[16] For their sympathy for the Muslim cause in Xinjiang, Beijing periodically protests to Turkey, Uzbekistan, Saudi Arabia, and Kazakstan. But most neighboring countries are afraid to give assistance to Xinjiang rebels. "Uighurs and the local population in Xinjiang want the Turkic-speaking states to help them," said the Uzbekistan president in a candid moment in 1998. "If we support this aim, our relations with the great China might be destroyed tomorrow."[17]

On a trip to Xinjiang in 1997, I found a political atmosphere like eastern China during the Mao years. The radio and

[15] *Taipei Times*, Oct. 11, 1999.
[16] *Kaifeng* (Hong Kong), July 1996, 39–40.
[17] Becquelin, 2000, 71.

newspapers spoke of Mao Zedong Thought, "class struggle," and the danger of enemies undermining the PRC. The CCP's fear of national disunity reaches maximum intensity in Xinjiang. While in Turfan, in the central part of the province, I turned on the official TV News (there is no other) and heard an editorial in Chinese: "Every friend of ours in religious circles should recognize that only the Chinese Communist Party represents the interests of the people of all ethnic groups." This is the imperial voice, abstract, dogmatic, divorced from reality.

In 2001, Beijing detected its antiterrorist, pro-imperial opportunity in a crack in the logic of the U.S.-led war. President Bush and most Americans saw themselves striking against broad forces of unfreedom. Beijing saw the war against terrorism as a defense of the unity of China. In addition to the common interest in opposing Islam-influenced terrorism, Beijing benefited from a certain opportunism in America's eclectic choice of partners in the antiterrorist coalition. Non-democratic leaders were embraced by Washington, among them Pakistan's military dictator—and Jiang Zemin.

Jiang joined the antiterrorism coalition because he saw a chance to strengthen his control over Xinjiang and further his ambitions to take Taiwan. In Kashgar, Yining, and other Xinjiang cities, where Muslims, as a gesture of dissent, set their watches two hours earlier than Chinese imperial time laid down by Beijing, hearts sank as Jiang joined the antiterrorist drive in 2001, declaring that the world might finally grasp China's "splittist" problem in Xinjiang.

Xinjiang and Taiwan! Separated by two thousand miles, like bookends on either side of China proper, of which both are wary. Chalk and cheese in way of life, economic structure, and standard of living. One attuned to Mecca and the call of the minaret, the other to the capitalist zones of the Pacific. But the Communist Party in Beijing sees itself as the rightful ruler of both.

The two bookends adopt opposite strategies toward Beijing. Taiwan advances separatism without overtly questioning Chinese imperial unity. Uighur militants seek separation, some using violent methods, while objecting to Chinese imperial unity, but so far without success. Abdulhekim of the East Turkistan Center in Istanbul has signaled that trouble in the Taiwan Strait would be accompanied by uprising in Xinjiang. "If China attacks Taiwan at four o'clock in the morning," he said, "we will have an uprising at three o'clock."[18]

As of this writing, we do not know how enduring the new post-9/11 political reality will be. The PRC is by no means in the terrorist camp. But neither is it in the liberal and democratic camp, the chief target of Al Qaeda. For the CCP, the place of Xinjiang, Tibet, and Taiwan as building blocks within the PRC has nothing to do with the wishes of the people in those "provinces"; it is not a project from below but an imperative from above. Time will tell whether Beijing, where the untested Hu Jintao has taken over the top CCP post from Jiang Zemin, really can use Bush's antiterrorist war to solidify the new Chinese Empire.

[18] *Taipei Times*, Oct. 11, 1999.

One Way China Responds to Dissidents Is by "Disappearing" Them

Michael Wines

In the following viewpoint, Michael Wines examines one of the methods China's government uses to silence opposition: removing any opponents from mainstream society by simply "disappearing" them. These methods include forced internment, a term in a prison camp, or perhaps even death, although some people "reappear" into ordinary life. As Wines notes, the families and acquaintances of those who have disappeared generally have no idea what has happened. He also explains that such measures violate international human rights agreements that China has promised to support. But alarmingly, Wines asserts, China is changing its legal system to allow the police to continue these practices. Wines is the China bureau chief for the New York Times.

Last Jan. 27 [2011], an Inner Mongolian rights activist, Govruud Huuchinhuu, suddenly vanished after leaving a hospital where she had undergone treatment for cancer. On Feb. 16, the Beijing human-rights lawyer Tang Jitian vanished after being forcibly taken away by police officers. On May 30, an ethnic Uighur, Ershidin Israel, vanished after being deported to China from Kazakhstan as a terrorism suspect. In the next two weeks, three other Uighurs vanished as well.

The Beijing artist and dissident Ai Weiwei, who vanished into police custody on April 3 and did not emerge until June 22, is but the most famous Chinese activist to suffer an "enforced disappearance," as human rights officials call such episodes. Experts say 2011 has seen a sharp and worrisome increase inside China of a security tactic that a United Nations international convention has sought to outlaw.

Rewriting the Law

Now China is answering complaints by rights activists that the disappearances of those and other Chinese are unlawful and potentially inhumane: It is rewriting the national criminal procedure code to make them legal.

The new proposal, drafted by a committee of the National People's Congress, the nation's quasi-legislature, is undergoing public review. It would amend the current code, which allows government authorities to place criminal suspects under house arrest for up to six months. The proposed revision would allow them to imprison in a secret location anyone who, under home surveillance, is found to hinder an investigation. Suspects' families would have to be told of their disappearance within 24 hours—unless doing so would hinder the investigation of crimes involving national security or terrorism.

Critics described the proposed revision as one of the most explicit backward steps in legal protections for people who offend the Chinese authorities since the country began moving toward the semblance of a Western-style legal system three decades ago. It would give security officials wide leeway to "disappear" dissidents and other activists without telling anyone—in other words, it would legalize Chinese officials' current practices.

"China, Death Penalty," cartoon by Rainer Hachfeld, *Neues Deutschland*, Germany, March 30, 2010. www.PoliticalCartoons.com. Copyright © 2010 by Rainer Hachfeld, Neues Deutschland, Germany, and www.PoliticalCartoons.com. All rights reserved.

New Procedures Could Protect Human Rights

The proposal is part of a larger revision of the criminal procedural code that has in other respects won praise from some legal experts, because it would give many ordinary criminal suspects new legal protections and rein in the ability of the authorities to commit abuses.

For example, the proposed text, which has just been published, appears to bar the use of evidence obtained by torture. It would give most criminal suspects an unqualified right to see a lawyer, and would extend requirements that witnesses actually appear at trials to give testimony.

While these are basic tenets of criminal procedure elsewhere, they are potentially groundbreaking advances in China, where the court system is not an independent branch of government, but rather answers to the Communist Party, whose overriding concern is maintaining state power.

It remains to be seen whether the revisions, if they are enacted, will be implemented as written. Some analysts have expressed skepticism that a ban on evidence obtained by torture could be effective, for example, because lawyers do not yet have the right to be present at interrogations, when most torture occurs.

"The balance between using the law to protect society and using the law to protect individual rights is still heavily weighted on the side of protecting society," said Joshua Rosenzweig, an independent human rights analyst based in Hong Kong and a leading expert on China's criminal procedure. "And, one could more cynically say, on the side of protecting the party."

Turning Dissidents into Criminals

If the past is any indication, the proposed revisions concerning forced disappearances are likely to affect a relatively small number of people, mostly dissidents and other thorns in the state's side. But their narrow impact does not reduce their significance, Mr. Rosenzweig argued.

Enforced disappearances are widely regarded as human-rights abuses because they deny suspects legal protections, needlessly subject relatives of the disappeared to mental strain and generally increase the chances that unsupervised officials who hold captives in undisclosed locations will engage in torture. Liu Xiaoyuan, a prominent defense lawyer known for his involvement in controversial cases, called the proposed revision "just scary."

"It literally gives the police a ticket to free themselves from any form of supervision," he said. "The criminal law should protect citizens' rights and restrict the power of the authorities. The new revision does exactly the opposite."

Caixin, an intrepid investigative business magazine, called the provision a "grab-bag justification that would lead to investigative organs being able to decide as they please whether or not to inform family members, and to secret detentions running rampant."

Dissident Liu Xiaobo

In 2010 Chinese dissident Liu Xiaobo was awarded the Nobel Peace Prize for his continued willingness to advocate on behalf of human rights and democracy and for his participation in the publication of Charter 08, a political manifesto created by more than three hundred Chinese activists and thinkers. The Chinese government strongly objected to the award, going so far as to censor news and broadcasts of the award ceremony.

Liu was born in 1955. Slightly young to be a Red Guard during the Cultural Revolution, Liu emerged as a literary scholar and critic in the late 1970s and 1980s. Known for making radical statements, he acquired a reputation as a freethinker and political activist. Liu was a leader during the 1989 Tiananmen Square protests and was eventually jailed for his participation, losing his university teaching job as well. A strong advocate of international justice and individual rights, Liu was jailed twice more in the 1990s, the second prison term taking place in a labor camp.

The proposal has not been approved, and could still change, although most experts consider that highly unlikely. Already, it has been the object of vigorous public criticism on some of the nation's major microblogs; one post charged that it had "pushed the Chinese people's sense of insecurity to a new height." Another post said, "The new criminal law should be called 'special people-controlling regulations for chaotic times.'"

An Emerging Controversy

Some analysts said they saw progress of a sort in the criticism. "Chinese citizens today no longer take it as a matter of course that the government has a God-given right to draw up any law it pleases," said Nicholas Bequelin, a researcher for Human Rights Watch who is based in Hong Kong.

Despite being declared a "subversive" by the Chinese government, Liu remained an active author and critic. He has written numerous books, including *Future of Free China Exists in Civil Society* and *Single Blade, Poisonous Sword: Criticism of Chinese Nationalism.* These books were published in the United States, because Liu's writings are banned in China.

Liu's most recent arrest took place because of his participation in the writing of Charter 08. Placed on trial in 2009 for "spreading a message to subvert the country and authority," he received a prison term of eleven years, which he is currently serving. His wife was placed under house arrest. Liu's detainment and sentence inspired protests from literary groups and governments around the world, including the United States.

In 2010, Liu was awarded the Nobel Peace Prize in absentia, unable to attend the ceremony in Oslo, Norway, due to his imprisonment. Local diplomats from a number of countries in Oslo declined to attend the ceremony, likely due to lobbying from China. While censoring news reports and restricting the movements of other known dissidents, China publicized instead a local version of the Nobel Prize, the Confucian Peace Prize.

In June, a United Nations working group on enforced disappearances expressed growing concern about the rise in such cases inside China, calling them "the continuation of a disturbing trend in the suppression of dissidents."

"There can never be an excuse to disappear people, especially when those persons are peacefully expressing their dissent with the government of their country," the group said in a written statement.

Two United Nations conventions, one enacted in 1976 and the other last December, commit member nations to refrain from making their citizens disappear in this way and to protect their legal rights. China has pledged to ratify both conventions, but has yet to do so. Nor has the United States ratified the 2010 convention, which explicitly prohibits enforced disappearances.

Like Mr. Ai, many of China's disappeared eventually resurface, some showing signs of having undergone arduous treatment while in captivity. Others have vanished without explanation for extended periods, including the Nobel Prize winning writer and dissident Liu Xiaobo, who vanished for six months in 2008 and 2009.

And some do not return at all, like the prominent human-rights lawyer Gao Zhisheng, who has not been heard from since he disappeared in April 2010. A handful have been missing for far longer.

CHAPTER 2

Controversies Surrounding the People's Republic of China

Chapter Exercises

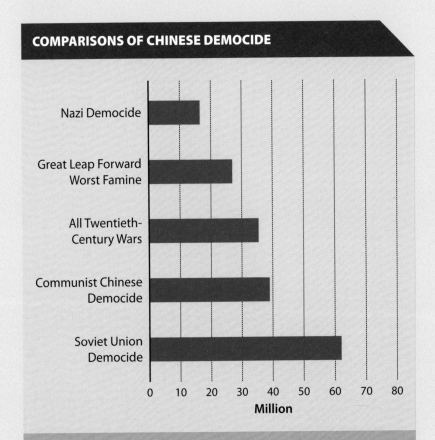

COMPARISONS OF CHINESE DEMOCIDE

Categories (top to bottom): Nazi Democide; Great Leap Forward Worst Famine; All Twentieth-Century Wars; Communist Chinese Democide; Soviet Union Democide

X-axis: Million — 0, 10, 20, 30, 40, 50, 60, 70, 80

1. Analyze the Graph

This chart compares various democides, or episodes of large-scale deaths, from different sources such as warfare, government policies, and famine.

Question 1: The Soviet Union was a Communist regime, as is the People's Republic of China. According to the chart, approximately how many millions of people died under these regimes?

Question 2: Compare how many people died under Nazi Germany (perhaps the most famous example of democide) to the victims of Communist Chinese democide.

Question 3: Combine the deaths from the Great Leap Forward famine and the Communist Chinese democide. How does the total compare to the other events on the graph?

2. Writing Prompt

Write an editorial examining how the status of China's ethnic minorities is being improved despite claims to the contrary.

3. Group Activity

Form two groups for the purpose of debate. One group should argue that the Great Leap Forward and Cultural Revolution were great tragedies for China. The other should argue that both events were part of the country's long process of learning and evolution.

Mao's Great Leap Forward "Killed 45 Million in Four Years"

Arifa Akbar

Until recently, it was hard for researchers to get access to official Chinese government documentation about the years of the Great Leap Forward. In the following article, Arifa Akbar reports how one such researcher, Frank Dikötter, has taken advantage of the Chinese government's new willingness to open up its archives. Dikötter, in a recent book on the subject, argues that the Great Leap Forward resulted in the deaths of 45 million people in four years from starvation, overwork, and government repression. The scale of the disaster suggests that the Great Leap Forward ranks with other tragedies such as World War II, in which 55 million people died. Akbar is an arts correspondent for the London Independent. *Dikötter is chair and professor of the humanities at the University of Hong Kong and the author of* Mao's Great Famine.*

Speaking at *The Independent* Woodstock Literary Festival, Frank Dikötter, a Hong Kong-based historian, said he found that during the time that Mao was enforcing the Great Leap Forward in 1958, in an effort to catch up with the economy of the Western world, he was responsible for overseeing "one of the worst catastrophes the world has ever known".

Mr Dikötter, who has been studying Chinese rural history from 1958 to 1962, when the nation was facing a famine, compared the systematic torture, brutality, starvation and killing of Chinese peasants to the Second World War in its magnitude. At least 45 million people were worked, starved or beaten to death in China over these four years; the worldwide death toll of the Second World War was 55 million.

Mr Dikötter is the only author to have delved into the Chinese archives since they were reopened four years ago. He argued that this devastating period of history—which has until now remained hidden—has international resonance. "It ranks alongside the gulags and the Holocaust as one of the three greatest events of the 20th century. . . . It was like [the Cambodian Communist dictator] Pol Pot's genocide multiplied 20 times over," he said.

Between 1958 and 1962, a war raged between the peasants and the state; it was a period when a third of all homes in China were destroyed to produce fertiliser and when the nation descended into famine and starvation, Mr Dikötter said.

His book, *Mao's Great Famine: The Story of China's Most Devastating Catastrophe*, reveals that while this is a part of history that has been "quite forgotten" in the official memory of the People's Republic of China, there was a "staggering degree of violence" that was, remarkably, carefully catalogued in Public Security Bureau reports, which featured among the provincial archives he studied. In them, he found that the members of the rural farming communities were seen by the Party merely as "digits", or a faceless workforce. For those who committed any acts of disobedience, however minor, the punishments were huge.

State retribution for tiny thefts, such as stealing a potato, even by a child, would include being tied up and thrown into a pond; parents were forced to bury their children alive or were doused in excrement and urine, others were set alight, or had a nose or

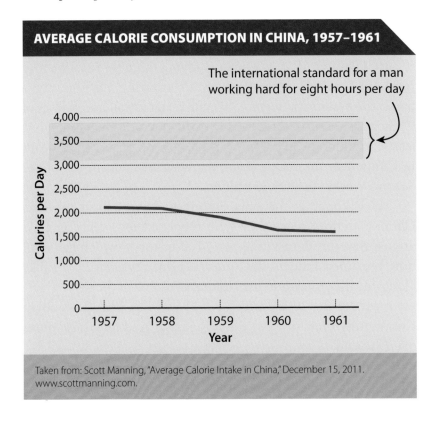

AVERAGE CALORIE CONSUMPTION IN CHINA, 1957–1961

The international standard for a man working hard for eight hours per day

Taken from: Scott Manning, "Average Calorie Intake in China," December 15, 2011. www.scottmanning.com.

ear cut off. One record shows how a man was branded with hot metal. People were forced to work naked in the middle of winter; 80 per cent of all the villagers in one region of a quarter of a million Chinese were banned from the official canteen because they were too old or ill to be effective workers, so were deliberately starved to death.

Mr Dikötter said that he was once again examining the Party's archives for his next book, *The Tragedy of Liberation*, which will deal with the bloody advent of Communism in China from 1944 to 1957.

He said the archives were already illuminating the extent of the atrocities of the period; one piece of evidence revealed that 13,000 opponents of the new regime were killed in one region alone, in just three weeks. "We know the outline of what went on but I will be looking into precisely what happened in this period, how it happened, and the human experiences behind the history," he said.

Mr Dikötter, who teaches at the University of Hong Kong, said while it was difficult for any historian in China to write books that are critical of Mao, he felt he could not collude with the "conspiracy of silence" in what the Chinese rural community had suffered in recent history.

China's Great Leap Forward Was Based on High Ideals but Had Unexpected Consequences

William Harms

In the following viewpoint, William Harms writes of China's Great Leap Forward, lasting from 1957 to the early 1960s. During this time, China's Communist government led by Mao Zedong tried to transform both industry and agriculture in hopes of turning the nation into an economic powerhouse. As Harms writes, this attempted transformation came at a huge cost. Using the memories and scholarship of University of Chicago professor Dali Yang, Harms reports how Chinese people were forced to work on large agriculture communes, devote themselves to large construction projects, and produce iron and steel in their backyards. Bad management and unrealistic goals helped bring about famines that killed millions, while hundreds of thousands of others were killed or imprisoned for resisting. The Great Leap Forward continues to exercise an important influence on China, Yang reports. Harms is the associate news director at the University of Chicago News Office.

As a child growing up in rural China, Dali Yang, Assistant Professor in Political Science, heard the stories of his par-

William Harms, "China's Great Leap Forward," *University of Chicago Chronicle*, vol. 15, no. 13, March 14, 1996. http://chronicle.uchicago.edu. Copyright © 1996 by University of Chicago. All rights reserved. Reproduced by permission.

ents and others about the horrors of the Great Leap Forward, a time of suffering for China that came soon after the Communist revolution in 1949.

"My parents were peasants who worked in the field. We grew wheat in the area where I lived, and they were part of a production team," said Yang, who was born in 1964, three years after the Great Leap Forward had ended. "They would often bring up the topic of the Great Leap famine and tell how bad things were during that time."

Yang's curiosity about the period led him to write the book *Calamity and Reform in China: State, Rural Society and Institutional Change Since the Great Leap Famine*, to be published this spring by Stanford University Press. The book, one of the first major works to analyze the period, relates how the Great Leap Forward and the subsequent famine still influence China today.

Unlike the later Cultural Revolution, which is well known in the West, the Great Leap Forward has been less of a focus for research by Western scholars—yet, according to Yang, it was one of the most influential periods of Chinese history. It was the pivotal event that led China to adopt reforms in rural areas after Mao's death in 1976, resulting in the dismantlement of the people's communes that the Chinese government had fervently advocated during the Great Leap Forward.

Communist Dream Leads to Mass Death

The Great Leap Forward was begun in 1957 by Chairman Mao Zedong to bring the nation quickly into the forefront of economic development. Mao wanted China to become a leading industrial power, and to accomplish his goals he and his colleagues pushed for the construction of steel plants across the country.

The rural society was to keep pace with the dream by producing enough food to feed the country plus enough for export to help pay for industrialization. As a result of the Communist revolution, landowners had been stripped of their property, and by 1957 peasants already were forced to work in agricultural cooperatives.

These changes were intended to improve conditions for everyone by collectivizing agriculture and establishing communal eating facilities where peasants could eat all they wanted free of charge. This utopian dream turned into a nightmare as the central leadership grew increasingly out of touch with reality, Yang found through his study of government records and personal accounts.

At the beginning of the Great Leap Forward, Mao proclaimed that China would overtake Britain in production of steel and other products within 15 years. Other Chinese leaders, including Deng Xiaoping, supported Mao's enthusiasm, according to documents Yang studied in China.

A year later, Mao radically revised the timeline for catching up to Britain—what was to be accomplished in 15 years now had to be done in just one more year, he said.

"Frequent changes in the timetable were symptomatic of the Great Leap, which, in retrospect, was fantasy incarnate. Even more exaggerated targets were subsequently presented, and then frequently revised upward, for steel, grain, cotton and other products. Any semblance of serious planning was abandoned," Yang said.

In pursuit of its goals, the government executed people who did not agree with the pace of radical change. The crackdown led to the deaths of 550,000 people by 1958.

The government also plunged the country into a deep debt by increasing spending on the development of heavy industry. Government spending on heavy industry grew in 1958 to represent 56 percent of state capital investment, an increase from 38 percent in 1956.

People were mobilized to accomplish the goals of industrialization. They built backyard furnaces for iron and steel and worked together on massive building projects, including one undertaken during the winter of 1957–58 in which more than

Commune residents used crude smelters, such as these pictured, to make steel as part of the goal of industrialization during the Great Leap Forward. © AP Images.

100 million peasants were mobilized to build large-scale water-conservation works.

Local leaders competed with one another to see who could create the most activity. In the rush to recruit labor, agricultural tasks were neglected, sometimes leaving the grain harvest to rot in the fields, Yang said. In the frenzy of competition, the leaders over-reported their harvests to their superiors in Beijing, and what was thought to be surplus grain was sold abroad.

Although in theory the country was awash in grain, in reality it was not. Rural communal mess halls were encouraged to supply food for free, but by the spring of 1959, the grain reserves were exhausted and the famine had begun.

No one is sure exactly how many people perished as a result of the spreading hunger. By comparing the number of deaths that could be expected under normal conditions with the number that occurred during the period of the Great Leap famine, scholars have estimated that somewhere between 16.5 million and 40 million people died before the experiment came to an end in 1961, making the Great Leap famine the largest in world history.

People abandoned their homes in search of food. Families suffered immensely, and reports of that suffering reached the members of the army, whose homes were primarily in rural areas. As soldiers received letters describing the suffering and the deaths, it became harder for leaders to maintain ideological discipline. Chaos developed in the countryside as rural militias became predatory, seizing grain, beating people and raping women.

From Famine to Reform

During the struggle for survival, farmers in nearly one-third of the rural communities took matters into their own hands, abandoning the people's commune in favor of individual farming. Heavy central control was reduced, and the country's agricultural production improved.

Following Mao's death in 1976, central leaders disagreed over rural policies. Taking advantage of this policy paralysis, peasants and local cadres made alliances in those areas that had suffered severely from the Great Leap Famine and contracted land to the farm household. In just a few years' time, the people's communes were dismantled. Agricultural performance improved dramatically and gave momentum to the reforms under Deng.

The memory of the famine reinforced the important role peasants play in China's development, Yang said. That memory also has undermined the appeal of central planning in rural policy-making.

"Historical developments during more than four decades of Communist rule in China have again and again shown us how the unanticipated consequences of elite policies subverted their attempts at fundamental social engineering," Yang writes in *Calamity and Reform in China*. Institutional changes in China are the result of a contest between the elite and the masses, between the state and the society, he said.

"This study thus points to the crucial importance of guarding against those who claim to know some magic route to the radiant future, be they politicians like Mao or party intellectuals who supported Mao or the new technocrats who claim to have found a scientific way to make China rich and powerful and who happily clamor for more power for themselves."

The best way to prevent the country from following another movement like the Great Leap Forward is to create mechanisms that check those in power, Yang said.

"Had there been a free press and other institutions of oversight that are commonly found in open political systems, the Great Leap famine would certainly not have attained the magnitude it did," said Yang, who continues to follow events in China through visits there as he develops his academic career in the United States.

The Cultural Revolution Continues to Cast a Dark Shadow over China

William A. Joseph

In the following viewpoint, William A. Joseph examines the Chinese Cultural Revolution. He writes that Mao Zedong's attempt to revive revolutionary enthusiasm was the result of an ideological struggle: the belief that elite interests remained dangerous even after a socialist revolution succeeded in the takeover of power. But Joseph also notes that the Cultural Revolution produced chaos, most notably in the actions of youthful Red Guards. Taking this as a lesson, China's leaders are fearful of new threats to public order and are ready to crush them quickly. Joseph is a professor of political science at Wellesley University and the author of many books, including The Critique of Ultra-Leftism in China, 1958–1981.

The "Great Proletarian Cultural Revolution" (1966–76) was launched by Chinese Communist Party (CCP) chairman Mao Zedong to stem what he perceived as the country's drift away from socialism and toward the "restoration of capitalism." The campaign, which was euphorically described at its inception by its progenitors as "a great revolution that touches people to

Adapted from William A. Joseph, "China's Cultural Revolution: A Brief Overview," in Joel Krieger, ed., with William A. Joseph, et al., *The Oxford Companion to the Politics of the World*, 2nd ed. New York: Oxford University Press, 1993, pp. 188–189. Copyright © 1993 by Oxford University Press. All rights reserved. Revised and reproduced by permission.

their very souls" and which inspired radical students from Paris to Berkeley, is now regarded as having been a terrible catastrophe for the Chinese nation.

The origins of the Cultural Revolution can be traced to the mid-1950s when Mao first became seriously concerned about the path that China's socialist transition had taken in the years since the CCP had come to power in 1949. His anxieties about the bureaucratization of the party, ideological degeneration in society as a whole, and the glaring socioeconomic inequalities that had emerged as China modernized escalated through the early 1960s and propelled him to embark on a crusade to expunge the "revisionism" that he believed was contaminating the party and the nation.

Continuing the Social and Ideological Struggle

Mao concluded that the source of China's political retrogression lay in the false and self-serving view of many of his party colleagues that class struggle ceased under socialism. On the contrary, the chairman concluded, the struggle between proletarian and bourgeois ideologies took on new, insidious forms even after the landlord and capitalist classes had been eliminated. The principal targets of Mao's ire were, on the one hand, party and government officials who he felt had become a "new class" divorced from the masses and, on the other, intellectuals who, in his view, were the repository of bourgeois [middle class] and even feudal [ancient landlord] values.

Mao's decision to undertake the Cultural Revolution was strongly influenced by his analysis that the Soviet Union had already abandoned socialism for capitalism. The Cultural Revolution was also a power struggle in which Mao fought to recapture from his political rivals some of the authority and prestige that he had lost as a result of earlier policy failures. Furthermore, Mao saw the Cultural Revolution as an opportunity to forge a "generation of revolutionary successors" by preparing China's youth to inherit the mantle of those who had originally brought the CCP to power.

Mao Zedong's widow, Jiang Qing (center), was arrested as one of the "Gang of Four" after Mao's death ended the Cultural Revolution. She was sentenced to death in 1981, and in 1983 her sentence was reduced to life imprisonment. She committed suicide in 1991. © AFP/Getty Images.

There was also a policy dimension to the Cultural Revolution: once those who were thought to be leading China down the "capitalist road" had been dislodged from power at all levels of society, a wide range of truly socialist institutions and processes ("sprouts of communism") were to be put in place to give life to the vision of the Cultural Revolution. For example, elitism in education was to be replaced by schools with revamped, politicized curricula, mass-based administration, and advancement criteria that stressed good class background, political activism and ideological correctness.

From the Red Guards to Mao's Death

The complex and convoluted history of the Cultural Revolution can be roughly divided into three major phases. The mass phase

(1966–1969) was dominated by the Red Guards, the more than 20 million high-school and college students who responded to Mao's call to "make revolution," and their often-vicious efforts to ferret out "class enemies" wherever they were suspected to lurk. During this stage, most of Mao's rivals in the top leadership were deposed, including China's president, Liu Shaoqi.

The military phase (1969–1971) began after the People's Liberation Army had gained ascendancy in Chinese politics by suppressing, with Mao's approval, the anarchy of the Red Guards. It ended with the alleged coup attempt in September 1971 by Mao's disgruntled heir, Defense Minister Lin Biao, who had also been one of the Chairman's main allies in launching the Cultural Revolution.

The succession phase (1972–1976) was an intense political and ideological tug-of-war between radical ideologues and veteran cadres [officials] over whether to continue or curtail the policies of the Cultural Revolution. Underlying this conflict was a bitter struggle over which group would control the succession to the two paramount leaders of the CCP, Chairman Mao and Premier Zhou Enlai, both of whom were in deteriorating health by the early 1970s. The decisive lot in this struggle was cast when the most prominent radicals (the "Gang of Four," which included Mao's widow, Jiang Qing) were preemptively arrested in October 1976, a month after the Chairman's death, by a coalition of more moderate leaders. The arrest of the Gang of Four is said to mark the official end of China's Cultural Revolution.

The Cultural Revolution is now referred to in China as the "decade of chaos" and is generally regarded as one of the bleakest periods in the country's modern history. The movement's ideals were betrayed at every turn by its destructive impulses. Hundreds of thousands, if not millions, of officials and intellectuals were physically and mentally persecuted. The much-vaunted initiatives that were to transform the nation often had disastrous consequences for China's education and cultural life. Economic development was disrupted by factional strife and misguided "ultraleftist" policies.

Lessons for Later Rulers

The market-oriented economic policies that China has followed since Deng Xiaoping came to power in the late 1970s represent a thorough repudiation of everything the Cultural Revolution stood for. Nevertheless the memory of the movement still casts an ominous shadow over Chinese politics. Deng, who was purged during the Cultural Revolution as one of China's leading "capitalist roaders," and the other elderly leaders who made the decision to crush the Tiananmen Square protests in June 1989 feared that, left unchecked, the demonstrations would snowball into Red Guard–like chaos. After Deng's death in 1997, his successors have continued to cite the experience of the Cultural Revolution as one of the reasons China cannot risk the disorder that democracy, by challenging Party authority, might bring to the country.

Chinese Leaders Learned from Both the Great Leap Forward and the Cultural Revolution

Zhao Huanxin and Zhou Wa

The Communist Party of China (CPC) celebrated its ninetieth anniversary in 2011, and it remains one of the few Communist parties in power and the only one that governs a major global nation. In the following viewpoint, a pair of Chinese journalists writes of a discussion with a professor, Xie Chuntao. Xie argues that one reason for the CPC's longevity is its willingness to learn from past mistakes such as the Great Leap Forward and the Cultural Revolution. Xie suggests that the human costs of these policies can be explained by international and local circumstances. More importantly, Xie argues, CPC officials were honest about their shortcomings and accomplished great things even during the country's most difficult eras. Xie is a historian working for the Chinese Communist Party's teaching division and is the author of Why and How the CPC Works in China.

Professor Xie Chuntao raises many eyebrows when he touches on certain topics, including why the Communist Party of China (CPC) remains popular despite making "several serious mistakes". The deputy director of the Party history division of the

Tourists gather for the Chinese Communist Party's ninetieth anniversary celebration in 2011 in Tiananmen Square. © AP Images.

Party School of the CPC Central Committee also explores issues such as why the CPC has not lost power like its counterparts in the former Soviet Union and Eastern Europe.

He asks these questions in the latest national best-seller— *Why and How the CPC Works in China.*

The book was published in March [2011], ahead of the 90th anniversary of the CPC that falls on Friday [July 1, 2011].

Highlighting Achievement and Errors

"It is natural that the 90th anniversary is celebrated with a show of achievements, that's why some people are 'stunned' that the book somewhat highlights the mistakes the Party made," Xie, who has studied the history of the Party for almost three decades, told *China Daily.*

"I don't think talking about the Party's errors will tarnish its image. Rather, it shows that the Party is straightforward and objective in its history," Xie, who compiled the book, said.

His work is one of the "red" books—publications about the communist revolution and socialist construction, which are taking up eye-catching slots on the shelves of bookstores across the country.

Sales of the 48-year-old professor's book outstripped most of the "red" books, with at least 200,000 copies sold since it was published, says Zhang Hai'ou, deputy editor-in-chief of New World Press, which published the book and is preparing an expanded edition as well as an English version of the book.

Xie writes that in the 20 years between 1957 and 1976, when leftist ideology was enforced, there had been almost no wage increases for workers and one out of four Chinese people often suffered from hunger. It was the period when the "Great Leap Forward" (1958–1960) and the turbulent "cultural revolution" (1966–1976) occurred.

In retrospect, the top CPC leaders then were pushing those movements out of "good motives" and "good will" amid complicated domestic and international situations, Xie writes.

The "Great Leap Forward" came about largely because, faced with oppressive pressure from the world powers, Chairman Mao Zedong believed China would risk being "dismissed from the earth" if it did not reverse its backwardness rapidly, the book reads.

In the same way, Mao had intended to build an ideal socialist society by starting a sweeping "cultural revolution", Xie writes.

"Good intentions, however, failed to yield good results; they were followed by wrong methods and actions," Xie said.

But even in those tumultuous years, the CPC was leading the way with economic and diplomatic changes that had long-lasting implications.

Development and Sacrifice

The country successfully tested its first atomic bomb in 1964, ended its dependence on oil imports in 1965, resumed its legal seat in the United Nations in 1971 and signed the Sino-US Joint Communique the following year.

The General Who Questioned the Great Leap Forward

In the years immediately following the Chinese Communist Revolution in 1949, leader Mao Zedong was largely intolerant of dissent, especially among high ranking officials who were supposed to reflect the unanimity of Mao's Communist vision. One respected official who did so, General Peng Dehuai, ended up paying a heavy price.

General Peng was one of the highest-ranking and most skilled military officers who fought on behalf of the Communist Party of China (CPC).

Always blunt and outspoken, Peng criticized Mao's policies during the Great Leap Forward on the grounds that they relied on vague ideals rather than on practical improvements. One of his chief concerns was the new emphasis on "commune armies" arising out

To overcome the ensuing hardship, senior CPC leaders went through thick and thin with the masses. A well-known anecdote goes that, in addition to reducing his salary, Mao gave up his favorite dish of pork braised in brown sauce during the famine years and had only a bowl of cornmeal porridge for supper on his 69th birthday.

At least 20 million workers who were lucky enough to work in cities during the "Great Leap Forward" returned to the countryside between 1961 and 1963, to show their understanding of the difficulties the country faced, the book reads.

But it was the leadership's acknowledgement of mistakes and learning from them that won the hearts of the people, Xie writes.

Mao assumed the primary responsibility for the "Great Leap Forward" and the central authorities categorically repudiated the devastating "cultural revolution".

of agricultural communes; Peng feared that they might undermine the increasingly professional People's Liberation Army. At the CPC's Lushan Conference in 1959, Peng made his concerns known not only to Mao but to other top officials. As a result, he was criticized as a "rightist" by Mao, stripped of all his official posts, and placed under house arrest. Another general, Lin Biao, replaced him as minister of defense.

Peng suffered greatly during the Cultural Revolution (1966–1976), as did many officials who were considered "right revisionists." He was a prominent victim of violent groups of Red Guards who, following a formal arrest, interrogated and beat him an alleged 130 times, injuring him severely. He was also subjected to public "Peng Dehuai struggle sessions," which featured beatings. Despite the charges against him, Peng continued to assert that he was loyal to China and its Communist future. Still under house arrest, he died of cancer in 1974. In 1978, after Mao's death and the repudiation of the Cultural Revolution, Peng was officially exonerated by China's new rulers. They publicly acknowledged him as one of the heroes of China's revolution.

"The Party's attitude was not to exaggerate glory and not to deny or evade failure as well as to learn from grave mistakes," Xie said. "That is still the case."

The second volume of *History of the Chinese Communist Party* (1949–78), published this year, devoted about 200 pages—nearly one-quarter of the total—to depict the Party's mistakes, including those in the "Great Leap Forward" and "cultural revolution" as well as their aftermath. It also analyzed the causes of policy failure and the misjudgment of Party leaders, Xie said.

Combating Corruption

In a chapter about how the CPC manages its colossal team of more than 80 million members—almost the population of Germany—Xie revealed that to become a Party member, one has to go through at least 17 procedures and is subject to about 100 rules and disciplines when admitted.

In recent years, at least 100 Party chiefs at the county level have been penalized for selling office appointments, Xie said. Rules have been put into place to avoid the over-centralization of power of officials at that level, he said.

Instituting regulations to tighten oversight is crucial for curbing rampant corruption, he said.

To combat corruption, the CPC needs to do something about the wages of officials and cadres, said Kerry Brown, a researcher with the School of Oriental and African Studies at the University of London.

"They have huge responsibility and very moderate remuneration. This is a recipe for corruption to thrive," Brown said.

Besides corruption, Xie's book also tackles other issues and difficulties challenging the CPC's development, including environmental problems brought by an extensive mode of economic development, and social problems such as the gap between the rich and poor.

Unlike other books on the Party's history, *Why and How the CPC Works in China* is full of stories with analysis and comments from foreign diplomats and experts, such as Kenneth Lieberthal, director of the John L. Thornton China Center and senior fellow at the Brookings Institution, and David Shambaugh, professor and director of the China Policy Program at George Washington University in the US.

"By collecting a wide variety of opinions, points made in the book are more insightful," Xie said.

Ending the Demonstrations in Tiananmen Square Was Necessary

Chen Xitong

The following viewpoint is part of an official Chinese government report on the violent crackdown in Tiananmen Square. Chen Xitong writes that the government had little choice but to declare martial law to end pro-democracy protests. He claims that his city had come to a virtual standstill, and foreign instigators were working together with criminals and radicals to keep the protests alive. While police and government officials exercised considerable restraint, Chen writes, their patience could not last forever if order was to be restored. Xitong is the former mayor of Beijing and former member of China's ruling politburo.

To safeguard the social stability in the city of Beijing, to protect the safety of the life and property of the citizens and ensure the normal functioning of the party and government departments at the central level and of the Beijing Municipal Government, the State Council had no alternative but to declare martial law in parts of Beijing as empowered by Clause 16 of

Article 89 of the Constitution of the People's Republic of China and at a time when police forces in Beijing were far inadequate to maintain the normal production, work, and living order. This was a resolute and correct decision.

The decision on taking resolute measures to stop the turmoil was announced at a meeting called by the central authorities and attended by cadres [officials] from the party, government and military institutions in Beijing on May 19. Comrade Zhao Ziyang [a top official], persisting in his erroneous stand against the correct decision of the central authorities, neither agreed to speak at the meeting together with Comrade Li Peng [Chinese premier] nor agreed to preside over the meeting. He didn't even agree to attend the meeting. By doing so, he openly revealed his attitude of separating himself from the party before the whole party, the whole country, and the whole world.

The Protestors Were Warned

Prior to this, members of the Standing Committee of the Politburo of the party's Central Committee met to discuss the issue of declaring martial law in parts of Beijing on May 17. On the same day, a few people who had access to top party and state secrets gave the information away out of their counter-revolutionary political consideration. A person who worked at the side of Comrade Zhao Ziyang said to the leaders of the illegal student organization, "The troops are about to suppress you. All others have agreed. Zhao Ziyang was the only one who was against it. You must get prepared."...

On the eve of declaring martial law and on the first two days after it was declared, all major crossroads were blocked. More than 220 buses were taken away and used as roadblocks. Transportation came to a standstill. Troops to enforce the martial law were not able to arrive at their designated places. The headquarters of the Party Central Committee and the State Council continued to be surrounded. Speeches inciting people could be heard anywhere on the street. Leaflets spreading rumors could be seen anywhere in the city. Demonstrations, each involving thousands of people, took place in succession, and Beijing, our capital city, fell into total disorder and terror. In the following few days, the martial law troops managed to enter the city by different ways. Meanwhile, the armed police and [the regular] police continued to perform their duties by overcoming tremendous difficulties. Urban and suburban districts organized workers, residents, and government office workers, as many as 120,000 people altogether, to maintain social order. The outer suburban counties also sent out militiamen. The concerted efforts of the troops, police, and civilians helped improve the transportation, production, and living order in the capital and people felt much at ease. But the very small number of people never stopped for a single day their activities to create turmoil and never changed their goal of overthrowing the leadership of the Communist Party. Things were developing day by day toward a counter-revolutionary rebellion.

In Tiananmen Square

One of the major tactics of the organizers and schemers of the turmoil after martial law was declared was to continue to stay on Tiananmen Square. They wanted to turn the square into a "center of the student movement and the whole nation." Once the government made a decision, they planned to make "strong reaction" at the square and form an "antigovernment united front." These people had been planning to stir up blood-shedding incidents on the square, believing that "the government would resort to suppression if the occupation of the square continues" and "blood can awaken people and split up the government."

To ensure that the situation on the square could be maintained, they used funds provided by reactionary forces both at home and abroad to improve their facilities and install advanced telecommunications devices, spending 100,000 yuan a day on an average. They even started illegal purchases of weapons. By using the tents provided by their Hong Kong supporters they set up "villages of freedom" and launched a "democracy university" on the square, claiming they would turn the university into "the Huangpu Military Academy of the new era." They erected a so-called goddess statue in front of the Monument to the People's Heroes. The statue was formerly named the "Goddess of Freedom" but its name was later changed to "Goddess of Democracy," showing that they took American-style democracy and freedom as their spiritual pillar.

Fearing that the students who took part in sit-ins could not hold on, Liu Xiaobo and other behind-the-scene schemers went up to the front stage and performed a four-man farce of a 48–72 hour hunger strike so as to pep the students up. They said, "As long as the flags on the square are still up, we can continue our fight and spread it to the whole country until the government collapses."

Taking advantage of the restraint that the government and the troops still exercised after martial law was declared, the organizers and plotters of the turmoil continued to organize all kinds of illegal activities. Following the establishment of the "Autonomous Students Union of Beijing Universities," the "Beijing Autonomous Workers Unions," the "Fasting Contingent," the "Tiananmen Square Headquarters," and the "Union of Capital's Intelligentsia," they set up more illegal organizations such as the "Patriotic Joint Conference of People from All Walks of Life in the Capital for Upholding the Constitution" and the "Autonomous Union of Beijing Residents." In the name of the Research Institute for Restructuring the Economic System, the Development Institute of the China Rural Development Research Center under the State Council, and the Beijing Association of Young Economists, they openly sent telegrams to some of the troops in an attempt to incite defection. They were engaged in such underground activities to topple the government as organizing a special team in charge of molding public opinion and making preparations to launch an underground newspaper.

The Chinese government's response to the Tiananmen Square clashes included sending tanks to the area. © AP Images/Jeff Widener.

Dangerous Demands and Careful Deceit

They organized their sworn followers in taking a secret oath, claiming "under no condition should we betray our conscience, yield to autocracy and bow to the emperor of China in the 1980s." Wan Runnan, general manager of Stone Company [a leading technology firm] listed the following six conditions for retreating from Tiananmen Square when he called together some leaders of the Autonomous Students Union of Beijing Universities in the international hotel: "To withdraw the troops, cancel martial law, remove Li Peng, ask [leaders] Deng Xiaoping and Yang Shangkun to quit, and let Zhao Ziyang resume his post." During the meeting, they also planned to organize "a great march to claim victory at midnight." Moreover, as they believed that there was almost no hope to solve problems without the party after Comrade Zhao Ziyang asked for sick leave, they pinned their hope on an emergency meeting by the Standing Committee of the National People's Congress [NPC].

Yan Jiaqi, Bao Zunxin [officials who supported the demonstrations], and others sent a telegram to the leaders of the NPC

Standing Committee, saying that "as the Constitution is being wantonly trampled by a few people, we hereby make an emergency appeal to hold an emergency meeting by the NPC Standing Committee immediately to solve the current critical problems."

Inspired by a certain member of the NPC Standing Committee, the Stone Research Institute of Social Development issued an opinion-collecting letter on the suggestion to convene such an emergency meeting. After getting the signatures of several members of the NPC Standing Committee, it sent urgent telegrams to NPC Standing Committee members outside Beijing. Conspiratorially, they said nothing about their true purposes in those letters and telegrams in an attempt to deceive those comrades who did not know the truth. They even went so far as to usurp the names of those comrades to serve their ulterior motives. . . .

Organizers and instigators of the turmoil also unbridledly agitated and organized actions of violence. They hooked up local hooligans, ruffians, and criminals from other parts of the country, ex-convicts who did not turn over a new leaf and people who have deep hatred of the Communist Party and the socialist system to knock together the so-called Dare-to-Die Corps, Flying Tiger Teams, Volunteer Army, and other terrorist organizations, threatening to detain and kidnap party and state leaders and "seize state power by means of attacking the Bastille [a reference to the French Revolution of 1789]." They distributed leaflets to stir up counter-revolutionary armed rebellion, advocating "a single spark can start a prairie fire" and called for establishing "armed forces that might be called the people's army," for "uniting with various forces including the Guomindang in Taiwan," and for "a clear-cut stand opposing the "Communist Party and its government by sacrificing lives."

They declared their desire to settle accounts with the party and the government after the event and even prepared a blacklist of officials to be suppressed. The Hong Kong-based *Ming Pao Daily News* published a "dialogue" on June 2 between Liu

Xiaobo, one of the organizers and planners, and "a mainland democratic movement leader," in which Liu said, "We must organize an armed force among the people to materialize Zhao Ziyang's comeback."

Foreign Influence and the Need for Strong Action

The activities of the instigators of the riots have strong financial backing. In addition to the materials worth some hundreds of thousands of yuan from the Stone Company, they also got support from hostile forces overseas and other organizations and individuals. Some people from the United States, Britain, and Hong Kong offered them nearly one million U.S. dollars and millions of Hong Kong dollars. Part of the money was used for activities to sabotage the martial law enforcement. Anyone who took part in establishing obstacles to stop traffic and block army vehicles could get thirty yuan a day. Also they set high prices to buy off rioters to burn military vehicles and beat soldiers, promising to offer three thousand yuan for burning one vehicle and more money for capturing or killing soldiers.

A high-ranking official from Taiwan launched a campaign to "send love to Tiananmen" and took the lead of donating 100,000 Taiwan dollars. A member of the Central Committee of the Guomindang in Taiwan suggested that 100 million Taiwan dollars be donated to establish a "Supporting Mainland Democratic Movement Fund." Some people of the Taiwan arts and cultural circles also launched "a campaign supporting the democratic movement on the mainland." A letter by the Autonomous Students Union of Beijing Universities to "Taiwan Friends in Art Circles" said that "we heartily thank you and salute to you for your material and spiritual support at this crucial moment. . . ."

All this shows that the turmoil planned, organized and premeditated by a few people could not be put down merely by making some concessions on the part of the government or just issuing an order to impose martial law, contrary to the imagination of some kind-hearted people.

They [had] made up their minds to unite with all hostile forces overseas and in foreign countries to launch a battle against us to the last. All one-sided goodwill would lead only to their unscrupulous attack against us and the longer the time the greater the cost.

Some Chinese Generals Refused to Participate in the Tiananmen Square Crackdown

John Garnaut

After declaring martial law in Beijing in May 1989 against protestors in Tiananmen Square, China's leaders decided to use the nation's military force, the People's Liberation Army (PLA), to end the event. By most accounts, what resulted was great violence, especially on June 4. But as John Garnaut writes in the following viewpoint, not all PLA leaders agreed to take part in the military crackdown. Some refused to obey anything but direct orders, while one officer refused an order to disperse protesters. Garnaut also notes that the stories of such officers remain largely hidden outside of personal memories and discussions among veterans. Meanwhile, the crackdown in 1989 remains such a painful and uncomfortable memory that both the Chinese government and the PLA marked its twenty-first anniversary with silence. Garnaut is an Australian journalist and the China correspondent for the Sydney Morning Herald *and* The Age.

In May 1989 the talented commander of the legendary 38th Army, Lieutenant General Xu Qinxian, defied an order from the paramount leader, Deng Xiaoping, to lead his troops to Beijing.

General Xu took no part in the subsequent killing of hundreds of protesters around Tiananmen Square, which is now quietly referred to in China simply as "June 4" and remains the worst incident of direct military violence against Chinese people in the People's Republic's 60-year history. The bloodshed split the People's Liberation Army [PLA] as it did the Communist Party and the country. "The case of General Xu is representative of the dissenting voice within the military," said Warren Sun, an authority at [Australia's] Monash University on the Communist Party's internal history. "Deng held a real fear of a possible military coup," he said.

The killings around Tiananmen continue to taint the legacies of the party elders who ordered them, led by Deng, and it weighs on the generation of mainly conservative leaders whose careers advanced because their more moderate colleagues were purged or sidelined at the time.

Those internal wounds are still raw, as demonstrated by the effort that the party and PLA have exerted to ensure today's 21st anniversary will pass without any public mention within China.

Conscientious Objectors May One Day Be Heroes

But acts of courageous defiance are kept alive by military and party veterans in private conversations and overseas Chinese language publications, in the belief or hope that those who refused to spill blood in 1989 will one day be acknowledged as heroes.

Around May 20, 1989, General Zhou Yibing, commander of the Beijing Military District, had couriered the marching orders to General Xu's barracks in Baoding, south of Beijing. "When he was ordered to march into the square, Xu asked a series of questions," said a serving general in the People's Liberation Army, answering queries from the *Herald* which were relayed via a close associate.

"He asked if there was an order from . . . Zhao Ziyang," said the serving PLA general, referring to the Communist Party boss who had already been sidelined because of his opposition to the use of force. The answer was no and "Xu then refused to march."

General Xu is the best known conscientious objector but not the only one.

On some accounts, General Xu's mentor, Qin Jiwei, who was then defence minister and a member of the politburo, attempted to forge an alliance with Zhao to oppose martial law. Zhao was purged and spent the rest of his life under house arrest.

"He was ordered to implement martial law [after a meeting at Deng's home on May 17] but he refused, saying he needed party authority," said a prominent scholar, whose father had served under Qin. "Qin called Zhao's office and waited for four hours until 2:30 in the morning to receive Zhao's return phone call overruling Deng Xiaoping . . . but the call never came."

There has been no public corroboration of this account by Zhao or those close to him.

The serving PLA general who responded to the *Herald's* questions about General Xu also pointed to the case of He Yanran, commander of the 28th Army.

"[General] He was also court-martialled because his armoured personnel carriers and trucks were burned down by angry onlookers and he refused to disperse them," said the serving general, through the mutual acquaintance.

General Xu was jailed for five years and is believed to be living a quiet life in occasional contact with reform-minded friends. General Qin later maintained a strong public show of support for the crackdown but was nevertheless deprived of his former power until his death in 1997. General He was demoted.

Chinese and Minority Explanations of a Uighur Riot Vary

Ariana Eunjung Cha

In July 2009, riots and demonstrations in Urumqi, the traditional capital of China's Xinjiang province, resulted in hundreds of deaths and injuries. In the following viewpoint, Ariana Eunjung Cha examines how the true causes of the violence remain a source of conflict and misunderstanding. Advocates for the Muslim Uighurs who make up the majority of the province blame Chinese government forces, while the Chinese government blames Uighur separatists organized by outside agitators. While both perspectives have their supporters, some observers suggest that the attempts to place blame, on both sides, are part of larger agendas. Most reject any serious implication, meanwhile, that Uighur activists have any clear ties to Islamic terrorist organizations in other countries, a claim put forward by the Chinese government. Cha is a reporter for the Washington Post.

Three weeks after the riots that left nearly 200 people dead and more than 1,700 injured in the capital of the far western Xinjiang region, the Chinese government and Uighur exile groups have been circulating dueling versions of what happened, in an emotional global propaganda war with geopolitical implications.

According to the version of events offered by China's Foreign Ministry and state media, the ethnic unrest that erupted in Urumqi [Xinjiang's capital] on July 5 [2009] was a terrorist attack by Uighur separatists. Women in black Islamic robes stood at street corners giving orders, and at least one handed out clubs, officials said, before Muslim Uighur gangs in 50 locations throughout the city simultaneously began beating Han Chinese.

In the account being circulated by Rebiya Kadeer, a U.S.-based Uighur leader who has emerged as the community's main spokesman, Chinese security forces were responsible for the violence that night. According to Kadeer, police and paramilitary and other troops chased peaceful demonstrators, mostly young people protesting a deadly factory brawl elsewhere, into closed-off areas. Then they turned off streetlights and began shooting indiscriminately.

Clear Details Absent

Chinese authorities have allowed foreign reporters access to the area where the clashes occurred and unusual freedom to conduct interviews, and they have provided evidence verifying the brutal attacks on Han Chinese. But few details are clear, and many witnesses who might be able to answer other questions—Who set off the initial violence? Why were the police unable to stop the attacks?—are either in jail or dead.

"The narratives of both the Chinese government and outside observers about what happened are hobbled by the lack of independent, verifiable accounts," said Phelim Kine, a researcher with New York-based Human Rights Watch, which is calling for a U.N. investigation into the incident.

Both sides face huge obstacles in trying to convince the world of their stories.

Violent protests broke out between Muslim Uighurs and Han Chinese in Urumqi in July 2009.
© Peter Parks/AFP/Getty Images.

The Chinese government, after decades of covering up and denying such incidents, has a major trust problem, many analysts say. Chinese officials have said they will release video footage of the attacks, phone records and other evidence to support their view of the events in Urumqi, but have not yet done so.

For [Rebiya] Kadeer, a 63-year-old former business mogul from Xinjiang who was exiled in 2005 and now lives in the Washington area, observers say the main challenge is convincing people that she can give an authoritative account of events that happened in a country she has not visited in years. Uighur exile groups have declined to provide information about their sources in China, saying they fear that those people will be arrested or worse if they speak out.

Resentment has been building for years between Han Chinese, who make up 92 percent of China's population and dominate its politics and economy, and Uighurs, who once were the majority in the far west, but whose presence there has shrunk in recent decades because of migration by Han Chinese.

Although the Chinese government says its policies have improved Uighurs' educational and job opportunities, some Uighurs say its goal is to assimilate them at the expense of their language, religion and culture.

Harsh Accusations

In the past, the government has linked Uighur separatism to a group known as the East Turkestan Islamic Movement, which it characterizes as a terrorist organization and blames for some recent attacks. Some analysts say that China exaggerates the influence of this group.

When it comes to the events of July 5, Dong Guanpeng, director of the Global Journalism Institute at Tsinghua University in Beijing, said he thinks China is being honest this time, but that doubts have been cast on the information it is releasing because Kadeer is "doing a better job than the Chinese government in public relations."

"Of course, Rebiya's statements have won sympathy in foreign countries," Dong said. "They contain beautiful lies."

Kadeer's version of events appears to have gained traction abroad. In Turkey, Prime Minister Recep Tayyip Erdogan has expressed solidarity with China's Uighurs, a Turkic-speaking minority group, and described the riots as "a kind of genocide." Protesters in Tokyo, Washington, Munich and Amsterdam have descended on Chinese embassies and consulates demanding a full account of what happened to Uighurs. A top Iranian cleric condemned China for "horribly" suppressing the community, and al-Qaeda's North African arm vowed to avenge Uighurs' deaths.

Zhan Jiang, a professor of journalism and mass communications at the China Youth University for Political Sciences, contends that the Chinese government inadvertently elevated Kadeer's status and gave her an audience that she does not deserve. Beijing has accused Kadeer of being the "mastermind" behind the clashes in Urumqi, accusations she denies.

"The government should haven't portrayed her as a hero by condemning her. She was unknown at first, and she is a well-known person in the world right now," Zhan said.

Gaps in Both Stories

Meanwhile, China has hit back by assigning some blame to third parties. The Communist Party's *People's Daily* newspaper said that the United States backed the "separatists" who launched the attacks. It also said that Kadeer's organization received funds from the National Endowment for Democracy, which in turn is funded by the U.S. Congress. Separately, the official *China Daily* has played up the terrorism angle, saying that the riots were meant to "help" al-Qaeda and were related to the continuing U.S. military presence in Afghanistan.

Some analysts say there are holes in both sides' narratives.

For instance, according to Kadeer's timeline of events, the violence was triggered by police who "under the cover of darkness . . . began to fire" on the protesters. But witnesses have said the rioting began about 8 p.m. Beijing time, when the sun was still up in Urumqi, 1,500 miles west of Beijing.

Chang Chungfu, a specialist in Muslim and Uighur studies at the National Chengchi University in Taiwan, said "the two parties—the government and Kadeer—are choosing the parts of the stories that favor their own agendas," in efforts to win foreign sympathy.

He said he considers it "unlikely that a peaceful protest turned into violence against innocent people just because of policemen cracking down," suggesting at least a measure of organization to the Uighurs' attacks on Han Chinese that night.

On the other hand, Chang said, he is skeptical of the government's assertions that Kadeer instigated the attacks because she lacks that kind of power. Furthermore, he said, "the government hasn't released detailed information of those who were killed, such as their ages and identities, so even the number of dead is in doubt."

Li Wei, a terrorism expert at the China Institutes of Contemporary International Relations, which is affiliated with China's national security bureau, dismissed allegations by state media of involvement by outside terrorist groups. "I have not found any proof that points at linkage between the riot and other terrorism groups, including al-Qaeda," he said.

Li did say, however, that he believes Kadeer is in contact with the East Turkestan Islamic Movement.

Rohan Gunaratna, a Singapore-based terrorism expert, blamed some of the tension on Beijing's failure to differentiate "between terrorists who attack and the political activities of separatists."

"If China is too hard on the Uighur people, then support of terrorism will grow," Gunaratna said. "The Chinese government must be hard on terrorists but soft on the Uighur people."

The Chinese Government's Investment in Its Minority Population Is Appreciated by Some Minority Group Members

Xinhua

The following viewpoint reports on the Communist Party of China (CPC) Central Committee's decision to invest more in the economic and social development of the Xinjiang region that is home to a large Uighur population. In addition to education about ethnic unity, investment will include tax breaks to impoverished locals, location of banks, and approval of undeveloped land for construction to improve the income and livelihood of the people of the region. Xinhua is the official news agency of the People's Republic of China.

The Chinese central authorities have set down strategic plans for far western Xinjiang Uygur Autonomous Region to achieve leapfrog development and lasting stability.

At a central work conference on Xinjiang's development concluded Wednesday, President Hu Jintao said Xinjiang should embark on a development path with Chinese characteristics and one that suits the region's situation.

Local traditional structures, such as this Uighur mosque, are being overtaken by modern architecture across the province of Xinjiang. © Carlos Spottorno/Getty Images News/Getty Images.

Despite Xinjiang's rapid development in recent years, it is still lagging behind the country's economically-developed eastern region due to various historical, natural and social reasons, he said.

Hu said the region should comprehensively push forward its economic, political, cultural and social development and enhance Party building under the new circumstances.

By 2015, per capita GDP in Xinjiang should catch up with the country's average level and the residents' income and their access to basic public services should reach the average level of the country's western regions, Hu said.

"Marked" improvement must be achieved in Xinjiang's infrastructure, self-development capacity, ethnic unity, and social stability within five years, he told the conference.

Xinjiang should fulfill the goal of achieving a moderately prosperous society in all aspects by 2020 by promoting coordinated

ETHNIC MINORITY POPULATIONS IN THE PEOPLE'S REPUBLIC OF CHINA

Census Year	Percentage of Total Population	Ethnic Population
1953	5.89	34,013,782
1964	5.77	39,883,909
1982	6.62	66,434,341
1990	8.01	90,567,245
2000	8.41	106,456,300

Source: Colin Mackerras, *China's Ethnic Minorities and Globalization*, 2003.

regional development. It should also improve people's living standards and build an eco-friendly environment, as well as ensure ethnic unity, social stability and security, he said.

Hu said managing Xinjiang well under the new circumstances is essential for improving the living standards of all ethnic groups. It is also a strategic imperative to ensure the development of the western region.

It is the common aspiration and responsibility of Chinese people of all ethnic groups to accelerate the process of building "a prosperous, harmonious and stable socialist Xinjiang," he said.

Hu noted that like other regions of the country, the society's principal problem is the gap between the fast growing material and cultural needs of the people and the low level of social production.

Hu vowed to invest more to improve the region's public services by implementing major projects to provide local people with a "modern and civilized" living environment.

He added resource development should be directly linked to the welfare of the local people.

Hu also called for comprehensive education about ethnic unity in order to help local people identify with the "great motherland, the Chinese nationality, Chinese culture, and a socialist development path with Chinese characteristics."

He urged efforts to oppose and strike down all ethnic separatist forces to ensure social order and people's normal life.

Hu said the supportive policies will also apply to the Xinjiang Production and Construction Corps (XPCC), a unique economic and semi-military government organization of about 2.5 million people, and pledged more government funding to boost its development and improve the social security of its employees.

Economic Support

At the meeting, Premier Wen Jiabao said the central authorities have decided to launch major support policies for Xinjiang, calling them necessary to accelerate the region's economic and social development.

He said Xinjiang will be the first region in China to start reform of resource taxes with a shift to taxing crude oil and natural gases by price rather than volume.

Under another tax policy to be introduced, qualified enterprises in impoverished areas in Xinjiang will be exempted from income tax for two years and allowed a 50 percent reduction for another three years, Wen said.

He said Xinjiang and the XPCC will continue to enjoy preference in receiving central government investment, which will more than double the total investment in fixed assets in Xinjiang over the next five years compared to the previous period.

The government will encourage joint-equity commercial banks, foreign banks, and banks of various kinds to open outlets and branches in remote areas in Xinjiang, he said.

China's Official Policies Toward Ethnic Minorities

About 8.5 percent of China's population consists of ethnic minority groups. While some, such as the Tibetans and Uighurs, are fairly large, most of the country's fifty-five recognized minority groups are small in number. In 2009 the Chinese government issued its most recent statement of policy toward these minority groups in a white paper.

The white paper asserts that members of minority groups are equal to all other Chinese people, a principle established in the People's Republic's 1982 Constitution. They are to be protected under law and maintain the same rights and freedoms as mainstream Han Chinese, including freedom of speech, of the press, and of association. They also, the document notes, have obligations toward the Chinese people and state, such as obedience to its laws. Ethnic communities have the right to elect delegates to the National People's Congress, a consultative body, while their members are actively recruited to serve as government officials

Wen also said the government will appropriately approve more undeveloped land for construction and development and expand the scale of consumption of natural gas in Xinjiang.

He stressed the first and foremost goal of the policies are to "ensure and improve the well-being of the people in Xinjiang."

All the nine members of the Standing Committee of the Political Bureau of the Communist Party of China (CPC) Central Committee—Hu Jintao, Wu Bangguo, Wen Jiabao, Jia Qinglin, Li Changchun, Xi Jinping, Li Keqiang, He Guoqiang and Zhou Yongkang—attended the conference.

The *People's Daily*, the CPC's flagship newspaper, will carry an editorial Friday outlining the central government's plans for Xinjiang's leapfrog development.

or bureaucrats. The white paper goes on to acknowledge that ethnic discrimination in any form is a violation of the law, in accordance with international conventions.

China's government also claims to protect and defend the unique religions, languages, and "folkways" of ethnic communities, asserting that each has the right and freedom to observe its own cultures and traditions. It cites, for instance, the presence of twenty-three thousand mosques in Xinjiang, the region mainly inhabited by Muslim Uighurs, as well as seventeen thousand places of worship for Tibetan Buddhists. Meanwhile, state-run newspapers and broadcasting stations use nearly one hundred different languages.

Underlying the government's policies is the principle of the unity of all groups in China under a single regime. For some members of ethnic minorities, including activists, this emphasis has led to challenges that contradict the official position of 2009's white paper. In ethnic areas, for example, the mainstream Mandarin language is becoming more commonplace and expected of residents. In addition, China's economic expansion has brought with it the establishment of institutions that reflect the dominant culture. Meanwhile, members of ethnic minorities continue to complain of discrimination when in contact with officials or when visiting areas of the country dominated by the Han majority.

Demonstration of Unity

"Such a top-level meeting on Xinjiang is the first of its kind to be held since New China was founded. It laid out an all-embracing blueprint for Xinjiang's future, and will play a significant role in boosting the region's development, stability and the border areas' security," said Hao Shiyuan, an expert on ethnology and anthropology and deputy secretary-general of the Chinese Academy of Social Sciences.

"I believe only in China, with its socialist system, can the central government mobilize all the nation's finances, resources and manpower to support a single region's development," said Hao, also president of the Chinese Ethnological Society.

"The combination of three sources—central government support, assistance from the economically developed provinces, and Xinjiang's self-development—demonstrates the spirit of unity and common endeavor. It will surely bring people of all ethnic groups in Xinjiang closer," he said.

Ma Dazheng, deputy director of the Research Center of China's Border History and Geography at the Chinese Academy of Social Sciences, said "while stressing the leapfrog development in Xinjiang's economy, the CPC Central Committee also underscores the region's overall development, such as education and personnel training."

"The people's livelihood is another major concern of the CPC Central Committee, which stressed bringing tangible benefits to the general public at the meeting. The people's livelihood is the foundation of development and stability," said Ma.

"Another highlight of the meeting is that the CPC Central Committee makes clear that Xinjiang's stability concerns the country's stability and Xinjiang's issue is more than a single region's issue. That's why the CPC Central Committee is to mobilize the strength of the entire Party and the entire nation to help Xinjiang achieve a leapfrog development," he said.

"The meeting gives us inspiring news," said Rayim Ismail, a resident of Uigur ethnic group in Urumqi, the regional capital of Xinjiang, Thursday.

He is moving from a shantytown to a new area in the city with better living conditions under a government-funded housing project.

"I am delighted to see more and more good policies issued for us," he said.

China Treats Dissidents Poorly

Gillian Wong

In the following viewpoint, Chinese dissidents argue that even if China allows activist Chen Guangcheng to leave the country, it will most likely not improve conditions for other dissidents. Many dissidents of the country see the possibility of Chen's departure as an individual victory and believe conditions for activists and dissidents within the country will continue to worsen. Despite what has happened with Chen, not all dissident issues can become an international concern, they maintain, and China's government power has no limits. Gillian Wong is a writer for the Associated Press.

Even if China makes a rare concession and allows legal activist Chen Guangcheng to leave the country with his family, other dissidents say they don't expect a broader easing of controls. Authorities might even tighten the screws on prominent critics to prevent them from taking encouragement from Chen's case to challenge the leadership.

The blind activist's escape from house arrest and flight to safety in the US Embassy has provided a much-needed morale boost for a dissident community that over the last year has been debilitated by a massive government security crackdown aimed at preventing an Arab-style democratic uprising. Dozens of activists, rights lawyers, intellectuals, and others have been detained, questioned, and in some cases, even tortured.

Chen, a symbol in China's civil rights movement, may be able to leave to study in the United States under still-evolving arrangements announced Friday by Washington and Beijing to end a weeklong diplomatic standoff over his case.

On Saturday, Chen was still in a hospital where he was taken to receive medical care, joined by his wife and two children. US Embassy officials met with his wife, although Secretary of State Hillary Rodham Clinton, in Beijing this past week for annual talks, left Beijing without visiting him.

The Foreign Ministry said Friday that Chen could submit an application to go abroad. His wife told Hong Kong broadcaster TVB on Saturday that applications for travel documents had not yet been started and no date has been set for them to leave.

The turn of events for Chen, while welcomed by most activists and dissidents, is seen as an individual victory that is not likely to pave the way for improvements in the government's attitude toward its critics.

"I think that after the Chen Guangcheng incident, the situation for us will just become worse and worse, because in today's society government power has no limits," said Liu Yi, an artist and Chen supporter who was assaulted Thursday by men he thinks were plainclothes police while he attempted to visit Chen in the hospital.

Liu Feiyue, a veteran activist who runs a rights monitoring network in the central province of Hubei, noted the importance of US involvement in Chen's case. "This is only an individual case. Because it turned into a China-US incident, the US put a lot of pressure on China, which is why the authorities made a concession to allow Chen Guangcheng to study overseas," he said.

"Not all dissident cases can become international issues," Liu Feiyue said.

Chen, a self-taught legal activist, is best known for exposing forced abortions and sterilizations in his community in a scandal that prompted the central government to punish some local officials. His activism earned him the wrath of local authorities, who punished him with nearly seven years of prison and house arrest.

He made an improbable escape from his farmhouse in eastern China two weeks ago and sought refuge in the US Embassy in Beijing. After negotiations between US and Chinese officials, Chen left the embassy under arrangements to stay in China that were supposed to guarantee his and his family's safety. But he then changed his mind, prompting more talks that resulted in Friday's tentative deal that would let him travel to the US with his family for a university fellowship.

All this played out as Clinton, Treasury Secretary Timothy Geithner, and a slew of senior US officials arrived for meetings on trade tensions and global economic and political trouble spots. It also occurred as Chinese President Hu Jintao and most of his senior leadership prepare to step aside for a younger generation of leaders—a time the Communist Party is acutely wary of challenges to its authority and usually reins-in critics.

Activists said that while Chen, his wife and children are likely to find sanctuary in the United States, it is unclear what will happen to his other relatives. Authorities have already detained Chen's elder brother, and his nephew is on the run after attacking local officials who raided his house apparently in search of Chen after his escape. Chen's mother, who lived with the couple, has been under constant surveillance.

If Chen leaves, the officials who mistreated him and his family will likely not be held accountable—something Chen asked for in a video statement he made while in hiding in Beijing before entering the US Embassy.

"Chen's story is not a triumph for China's human rights, unfortunately," said Wang Songlian, a Hong Kong-based researcher with Chinese Human Rights Defenders. "Although Chen and his

Fang Lizhi, forced to flee China for his criticism of its leaders, became a professor of physics at the University of Arizona. Lizhi died April 6, 2012. While some Chinese dissidents have escaped the country, their individual victories don't benefit the human rights of other Chinese citizens, some critics argue. © John B. Carnett/Popular Science/Popular Science via Getty Images.

immediate family might gain freedom, his extended family is likely to be retaliated against. . . . None of those whose violence Chen exposed, or those who beat and detained Chen and his family, have been punished."

Score-Settling to Come?

There are concerns China will exact retribution on Chen's supporters who aided his escape, as well as friends who later tried to get the message out about his fears for his safety or publicly urged him to flee to the United States. Two supporters who helped him escape were detained, then released, but placed under gag orders and close monitoring.

Others like Chen's friend Zeng Jinyan, who—at great risk to herself—publicized Chen's worries about leaving the embassy Wednesday, have since been barred from speaking to the media and placed under house arrest. Also under similar restrictions is Teng Biao, a rights lawyer who repeatedly called Chen imploring him to flee the country, then published a transcript of their phone conversations online.

"They [the authorities] will certainly settle scores with them later," Teng told Chen, referring to the two supporters who aided Chen's escape.

Some activists say local officials who have been watching dissidents in their own jurisdictions might beef up monitoring and restrictions on them to prevent them from attempting copycat escapes into diplomatic compounds.

"One guess is that they will learn a lesson from this experience and be stricter in guarding and monitoring similar key figures and take even harder measures against them," said Mo Zhixu, a liberal-minded author and Chen supporter.

China's Human Rights Record Is Improving

Associated Press

In the following viewpoint, the Associated Press presents China's viewpoint that the United States needs to address its own human rights violations instead of attacking issues within China. Although the United States claims that the human rights record in China is poor, the Chinese Foreign Ministry contends that its progress and improvement on human rights is remarkable. The Chinese government maintains that the United States should stop depicting itself as a human rights watchdog.

Beijing (AP)—China responded Thursday to a U.S. report critical of its human rights record by releasing its own review attacking America's rights record as "tattered and shocking."

The State Council, or Cabinet, released the report two days after the U.S. State Department took China to task for widespread human rights violations.

China's report criticized violent crime in the U.S., its large prison population and the wars in Iraq and Afghanistan.

"It is high time for the U.S. government to face its own human rights problems with courage . . . and give up the unwise practices of applying double standards on human rights issues and using it to suppress other countries," the report said.

The U.S. Embassy in Beijing said that any U.S. comment on the Chinese allegations would be released in Washington.

Washington's report this week detailed China's increased attempts to control and censor the Internet and tighten restrictions on the media and freedom of speech.

"China's overall human rights record remains poor," the U.S. report said.

The U.S. report gave a chilling account of alleged torture in China, including the use of electric shocks, beatings, shackles, and other forms of abuse. The report also details claims by citizens forced from their homes to make way for Olympic Games projects in Beijing.

China has voiced strong opposition to the State Department report, saying China respects and safeguards human rights.

"The efforts and remarkable achievement China has made on the issue have already been widely recognized by the international community," Chinese Foreign Ministry spokesman Qin Gang said in a statement on the ministry's website.

"We suggest the U.S. government to stop depicting itself as a human rights watchdog and focus more on its own human rights problems," Qin said.

He said China was willing to have dialogue on human rights with the U.S. and other countries.

The tit-for-tat charges come less than five months before Beijing hosts the Olympic Games, which have already put the spotlight on China's human rights record.

The reports also come as the two countries' economies become increasingly entwined and amid increased political cooperation between the U.S. and China on international problems, including efforts to strip North Korea of its nuclear program.

Beijing's report, gathered from a variety of international news sources, lambastes an increase in violent crime in the U.S., saying it poses a serious threat to the lives, liberty and personal security of the American people.

The report concluded the U.S. human rights record is "best described as tattered and shocking."

It cited an FBI report on crime statistics in the U.S. released last year that showed violent crime had increased by 1.9% from 2005 to 2006, with 1.41 million cases reported nationwide.

The report also cited news articles that said 30,000 people die in the U.S. from gunshot wounds every year and gun killings have climbed 13% since 2002.

It noted the United States has the largest prison system in the world, with the highest inmates-to-population ratio. The report cited police brutality and other instances where law enforcement officials violated civil rights.

China's report also lambasted the U.S. for the wars in Iraq and Afghanistan.

"The invasion of Iraq by U.S. troops has produced the biggest human rights tragedy and the greatest humanitarian disaster in modern world," the report said.

It also said U.S. troops had killed innocent civilians in the anti-terrorism war in Afghanistan.

CHAPTER 3

Personal Narratives

Chapter Exercises

1. ## Writing Prompt

    Imagine that you are a prisoner in a Chinese labor camp. Write a one-page journal entry examining your day-to-day experiences.

2. ## Group Activity

    Form groups and come up with five interview questions you might ask victims of oppression in China. Consider such possible victims as members of ethnic minorities, anti-government demonstrators, and people caught up in such events as the Cultural Revolution or the Tiananmen Square crackdown.

Memories of a Political Prisoner from the Years of the Great Leap Forward

Zhang Xianliang

In the following viewpoint, Zhang Xianliang recounts his experience as a prisoner in a forced labor camp in the early 1960s. From a wealthy family, Zhang was already a poet when he was arrested and imprisoned in 1957 for having "rightist" sympathies. He remained a prisoner at various locations until 1979. Zhang notes not only his personal struggles but ways he and other prisoners tried to cope, such as discussing literature. He also mentions key features of China's Great Leap Forward. These include exhortations from leader Mao Zedong to "Work Bitterly Hard," when peasants not working hard enough could be imprisoned. Zhang's books include Grass Soup, Half of Man Is Woman, *and* Mimosa and Other Stories.

The end of 1960 was probably the worst time in my life. It is hard to imagine it now: we were at peace, there was no war going on. Why was it necessary to put thousands of men in the fields in drenching cold rain and make them stay out there to eat their meagre meals? It was not so very far to go back to the barracks—including eating, the whole lunch would have taken perhaps half an hour.

Exaggerating the Quota

Agricultural production was originally meant to provide convicts with our basic living requirements. Later, production came to be regarded as a number used to fill a target quota. Still later, production came to be something that was necessary to keep people from being idle. The results of production were measured simply by the fact that men were doing something. One only had to see everyone working, doing unending hard labour, to be able to declare that production was going up.

In fact, the rice that we raised was blighted and useless—many husks were empty. It would have been better to leave the rice stalks in the fields as fertilizer for the soil. But since our Great Leader [Mao Zedong], born of a peasant's family, could convince himself that one mou of land [about 1/5 acre] could produce one hundred and sixty thousand jin [about 176,000 pounds] of rice, blighted grain had to be included in our figures to make up the numbers.

So we worked night and day, taking no account of driving wind and rain. We were to 'work hard, work bitterly hard'. This was the exhortation promulgated by the Great Leader to his people. On 19 September, when the camp assembled all the convicts for the Autumn Harvest Mobilization meeting, Troop Leader Yan emphasized this slogan over and over again. 'Work Hard, Work Bitterly Hard.'

Mao Zedong was adept at modifying political slogans to meet the times. In 1958, when I had just entered the camp, what we were told was 'Work Hard, Work with Imagination'. This still allowed the intelligence and talents of intellectuals a little bit of room, something for which to aim. There was still just this little bit of respect for science and technology.

Hard Labor for Its Own Sake

By 1960, intelligence and talent were useless. Science and technology were also unnecessary, so that what was left was sheer physical labour. The mentality behind Work Bitterly Hard matched the slogan perfectly. In fact, only intellectuals responded to the different messages in the different slogans. If told to work ingeniously they would think up all kinds of clever ways and means, even inventing a new recipe for steamed buns that were made from rice straw. The more you ate, the faster you died. Told to Work Bitterly Hard, they would throw themselves into it, dredging forth their last reserves of strength; told to do something they would do it, and the more they did it the faster they died.

Criminal convicts learned not to accept this very early on. An example is Chen Yuzhong, that beggar of leftovers who on 1 October said indignantly that he would rather go to a proper official labour reform camp than this place. He told me that going to hell would be better than staying here. The standard Chinese approach to getting out of a tight spot is as follows: if the situation is not good among people, then see how it works in hell. If the first level of hell is no good, go to the second; if the second stinks, press on to the third. As for heaven? Don't even think about it. Naturally, we, too, have occasionally dreamed of a beautiful future, but it has too often turned into disaster. Experience has therefore trained us to think only in terms of bad things, never to dream for a better future.

Relieved by Heavy Rain

Suddenly, at this exhausted and traumatic time, doing labour that was utterly without significance or reward, there appeared an external force that operated on and controlled those who in turn controlled us. This power allowed us to sit at home, out of sight of bosses. We could even lie down and sleep. And so we came to have infinite appreciation for that external force, we came to hope for it every day.

That external force was no more than very hard rain. A drizzle wouldn't do, that would only increase your misery. It had to be buckets of torrential rain.

The heavier the rain, the happier the convicts became. They applauded it and rejoiced in it, but the rain had to fall during the daytime to be of any use. We had a proverb: 'Rain at night, clear in the day, makes a convict so mad his stomach burns.' The proverb is plain and direct, a good example of convict language.

A fondness for hard rain is something I have kept to this day. It has been thirty years since my first experience of a labour re-form camp. I now have work that I like, but every time I encounter a rainy day I put down my task, no matter how important, and go to sleep. The sound of rainwater rushing through the gutters of the eaves is the music I love most. That sound can send me into a frame of mind both melancholy and deeply content. It is distant and intimate, raucous and serene. In the swishing sound of rain, I either lie out straight in my bedding or curl up and let every nerve relax, let every cell in my muscles open. With exquisite appreciation, I feel the gladness in my heart and the relaxation of my body. At such times I can hear the various messages of nature passing through the rain. The humidity seeping into the room is a natural element between heaven and earth which gradually surrounds me, melts me, leads me to the state that ancient Daoists once sought. It takes me where the spirit is elevated to a point of not existing, where the open mind is at a pinnacle of awareness. Where, spoken or written, words fail to convey anything but a superficial understanding of what Daoists take as constituting the only element in the universe.

Because of the effect that rain still has on me, I don't in fact believe that people can so easily forget the past.

On 28 September it rained all night then kept on in the morning. The Troop Leader and convicts researched the bubbles stirred up by raindrops that were pummelling the puddles. If the bubbles immediately broke open, that meant the day would clear. If they floated here and there on top of the puddle, then it was certain it would continue to rain. According to this farmer's meteorological lore, it looked as if today it would be raining till nightfall. Convicts were therefore assigned to 'study while you plait together straw ropes'. Production and reform—one was not to miss out on either.

Plaiting ropes was easy and everyone worked away in high spirits. But by ten o'clock the farmer's lore began to fail and the rain diminished. The Troop Leader's copper whistle sounded shrilly through the yard once again. 'Everyone gather right away! Prepare to go out to work!' Making ropes was not considered work.

Like the burst bubbles, everyone's hopes evaporated but the only thing to do was to go out in the rain. Heads hanging low, we stomped along in the mud, weaving back and forth as we headed for the fields. Weary feet sloshed through muddy water; sucking sounds came from all directions. Fortunately the mud of the loess plateau is both finely grained and soft. It doesn't get too slippery and it doesn't stick completely to your feet—otherwise the entire line of men would have slipped and fallen, and never been able to get up again. These were men so feeble that they could scarcely raise their legs, never mind slogging through muddy fields.

As we walked along, the mountains in the west looked as though they were floating in black clouds. Finally the rain came down again. The convicts picked up interest; their mood improved. With hands hugging their shoulders they now stood still, neither moving forward nor daring to run back home. Looking this way and that like chickens stretching out quivering necks in the pounding rain, they silently waited for the Troop Leader's life-saving blow on the whistle.

By this time the whistle was clogged with rain. The Troop Leader tried but couldn't blow a real note, just a little breathy peep as though he and the whistle were sighing together in disappointment. Even that weak noise was heard through the rain and through the great expanse of nature. Instantly, like a startled flock of birds, the convicts flapped their wings twice and turned towards home.

There was not a dry place on us from head to foot. Like the Troop Leader's copper whistle, the cracks in our bones had been plugged with water. But consider how happy we were! Fate had decreed that we would have to work, but the old man in the sky had changed our fortune for that one day. While going from a drizzle to a downpour, the colours of the sky changed dramatically. The village in the distance, the fields, the wild wastes, the grasslands, the water in the canal all took on different hues as the weather changed. Behind the curtain of rain everything in life became less focused—so what were we racing back to do? Merely to plait straw ropes! Then why were we walking so fast? Let us stroll as if through a park!

Glorifying the Communist Revolution

It was then that Wang Sanyu and I began chatting, 'discussing literature and books'. He did not know much about Chinese poetry but said he liked the poetry of a particular Russian named [Mikhail] Isakovsky. I asked why. He couldn't really answer—perhaps it was because many of the poems had been turned into songs and could easily be remembered. 'Listen to one,' he said, and he began to sing.

> A small winding road narrow and endless
> Going towards the vast unknown
> I want to follow this long narrow road
> Follow my love who is going to war . . .

His singing voice had a deep timbre and was extremely soulful. His vocal cords and lungs were sturdier than any whistle made of metal; hunger and rain had not reduced the coloration of the sound he produced. The tune was melodious and gentle; his voice was given added resonance by the humidity. It called back a remembrance of a world that had not completely vanished. And what was that world? Naturally it included a red flag and battle. It was world revolution, one class overpowering another, liberating all of mankind. It was for that sacred enterprise that we were here reforming ourselves, harvesting rice, making straw ropes, eating millet gruel. The sacred enterprise could not be a mistake. Surely it was we who were mistaken. . . .

We talked about contemporary Chinese novels, and about how inspirational some of the famous sayings in Russian novels were. We walked beside a canal so full it flowed even with the banks, like a river, and although we were wet through we didn't mind, like when you're wet after swimming and it doesn't matter. We were glowing with idealism. We recalled that phrase in *Advance the Mother Country*:

> Where could you ever find another country
> In which people have such freedom to come and go?

How could we imagine anything else? From childhood we were fed on illusory spiritual nourishment. A shining and resplendent and oh-so-desirable but unattainable future was spread before us. We weren't taught how to defend our own individual rights, how to distinguish where our real interests and where the people's interests lay. A massive orb of light was hung over our heads and we were made to understand that this was the purpose of our whole life's struggle. We seemed to have our sights set far in the distance, on the future of mankind—but the circle of light blinded our eyes. From the big yard of the labour reform camps to the fields, and back again from the fields to the big yard was the precisely defined path that we were permitted to travel. We were not even allowed to go to the other side of the canal. And the villagers—what about their 'freedom'? I already knew that 'those who don't work hard will be sent to do labour reform', also that 'grass had already been dug clean by the local people'. Yet we truly did believe that sentence, 'Where could you ever find another country in which people have such freedom to come and go?'

Now, what country can you think of where people are really free?

The strange thing is that precisely because we thought we were being punished on behalf of an ideal, we did not feel that we were experiencing such great hardship. If it was to be millet gruel, all right, millet gruel. If we were to eat in the rain, fine, in the rain. Spiritual motivation and psychological deceit seem to be very much the same thing.

A Family Struggles During the Cultural Revolution

Yukui Liu

During China's Cultural Revolution (1966–1976) many families that lived in cities were forced to move to the countryside on the principle that rural life was more pure and productive than urban life. Former urbanites were sometimes forced to endure "struggle" or "self-criticism" sessions if they were deemed not strong enough in their revolutionary ideology. These sessions could go as far as tor-ture and sometimes even death. In the following viewpoint, Yukui Liu details how his family was sent to the countryside and his fa-ther became the target of revolutionary extremists. Liu, an exiled Chinese doctor of traditional medicine, lives in the United States and is active in the Falun Gong, a spiritual and health movement that actively opposes China's Communist government. The names have been changed to protect Liu and his family members.

I grew up in communist China during the Great Cultural Revolution. Life for Chinese people was bitter when the state-initiated "class struggle" swept through our country like a wild-fire of violence, lasting ten long years. Although the central fig-ure of this story is my father, the things perpetrated upon him affected our entire family. For me, the eldest son, the suffering and stress is still ever-present in my mind—as intended by this regime that uses extreme brutality to make examples of people in order to spread fear and subjugate the masses.

When I was six years old, in 1963, during a period called "Socialist Education Movement" just prior to the Cultural Revolution, our family was banished to a small village in northeastern China because my father had received a few years of Japanese education during World War II. The area we were sent to was poor and undeveloped, without transportation or electricity, and there were no jobs. My father was a university professor and suddenly had to become a farmer to support the family—my parents, grandmother, younger sister and myself. Since my father had never farmed before, we could not grow enough food on the countryside paddies, and we suffered much hunger during those years. My parents had no income, so my mom raised a few chickens to sell eggs so she could buy paper and pencils for me to go to school.

It was an unusually cold winter in the year of 1968, when I was 11 years old. It continued snowing every day, covering the village. We never saw the sun or the moon all winter, while enduring freezing cold days and nights of up to −30 degrees Celsius (−22 degrees Fahrenheit.) I was attending the village elementary school. One day, an event at school caused an unforgettable blow to my soul. As usual, I walked the two miles of snow-covered mountain road to school. But when I walked into my classroom, there was nobody there—no teacher, no students. Instead, the walls were covered with posters filled with Chinese brush characters in black ink. As a fourth grader I could already read all the Chinese characters, and I was startled by the content of those posters. They were all attacking my father, saying things like: "Overthrow counterrevolutionary Liu Shibao [the author's father]!"

A Father Is Persecuted

Scared and confused I walked around the campus and saw more of these posters everywhere, all over the school. I realized that many village people, including some students, had posted these.

This was in the third year of the Great Proletarian Cultural Revolution, a political movement launched by the Chinese communist party (CCP) in May 1966, to control and purge the educated elite, including teachers and scientists, through terror and persecution. This cruel and destructive movement in total lasted for 10 years and spread all over the country.

From that day on, my father was ordered to attend nightly public criticism meetings, also called "struggle sessions" (Pi Dou Da Hui or Pi Pan Da Hui in Chinese). Several hundred villagers were also ordered by authorities to attend and to "struggle" with the "struggle target" or "class enemy" by verbally, and sometimes physically, abusing him or her.

My father was labeled a "history counterrevolutionary" and was required to have that title pinned to his clothes on a card at all times, in public and at home. The criticizing meetings were organized by a Cultural Revolution Leading Committee, a special governing agency of the Communist Party. During the meetings my father had to kneel for over three hours while people berated him loudly and violently. People shouted over and over: "Beat down Liu Shibao! Beat down Liu Shibao!" Some people made up false stories about my father, making people hate him. Some people became very riled-up and out of control that they would spit at him and beat him.

With this kind of abuse being repeated over and over, night after night, my father was eventually nearing breakdown. He became sick and exhausted, always dizzy, with headaches, nausea, and sometime he nearly passed out. His emotions went between anger, fear, hate, hopeless, helplessness, and depression.

We were very scared and worried for my father. My grandmother was crying all the time. My mom and I were afraid that he might die. Every night before the struggle sessions started, my mom and I hid outside the meeting place. With temperatures at −22 degrees Fahrenheit, we were shaking from the cold, and our feet were painful and numb. Even so, we still kept staying there to listen to the meeting, and maybe help my father, should his situation become dire. My mom's plan was that if my father became too weak, we would go into the meeting room and kneel down in front of the village people, begging them to stop.

"If they still have a little bit of human heart left, they may stop, and we may be able to save your father's life," mom said.

The struggle session sometimes went on until midnight. After it was finally over, we helped my already exhausted father to walk back home. On the way home, we passed a well—the only well from which the village people got their water. My mom always worried if my dad walked home by himself, he might commit suicide by jumping into the well. This was another reason why my mom and I waited outside the meeting place during those freezing cold nights to take my father back home.

Such dark days and nights continued. Each struggle session produced more fake stories about my father, so people's hatred against him became ever more extreme. Those fake accusations were made up under pressure from the leaders of Cultural Revolution Leading Committee, the Communist Party members. Without providing any factual evidence, these fabricated reports were used to slander and destroy "the enemy." They were loudly read in front of the people and then posted on walls at school and all public places throughout the village, for everyone to see.

The frenzied and irrational mob-like environment of these class struggle meetings created such hateful energy that it even pushed people into a killing mood. Many innocent teachers, professors, engineers, scientists, and religious leaders were thus beaten to death. My father was facing this situation too. Our whole family was in fear that any day my father would be beaten to death. . . .

An Uncle Urges Escape

After painful mental struggle, my uncle decided to secretly come to our house and persuade my father to flee. My uncle had thus walked through the very heavy snow in the dark of night. He had to be very careful and quiet not to make any dogs bark. If anyone saw him going to our house, he would have been arrested right away.

We all sat on the floor in the dark room, listening to my uncle talk to my parents in a hushed voice: "Brother and sister, please take my words very seriously. They have already prepared everything to torture brother at tomorrow's struggle session. The only way to save yourself is to escape before daybreak, otherwise they will kill you. I finally decided to come tell you under risk of my own life. Now there are only a few hours left, so please hurry up and get ready to escape somewhere far away!"

After this, my uncle left quietly, and we hastily moved into action. My mom used the only two pounds of bread flour we had for the entire year to bake a few Chinese pancakes for my father to take along. I sat on the floor, helping my mom by keeping the wooden fire going.

We got my father ready to leave in about 30 minutes. All our family members, including my little sister and my grandmother, were crying as we said goodbye and watched my father gradually vanish into the darkness of the blizzardy night.

With just a few pancakes and 50 yuan my uncle had given him, my father left home in that cold winter night of 1968 to escape being beaten to death at the struggle session set up for the following evening.

A Quick Departure

My father had no time to think about leaving his wife, children, and old mother behind to fend for themselves as he needed to quickly decide which direction to take, and to get away from the village as quickly as possible so he would not be caught by militiamen who would be screening the area soon.

The snow was higher than his thigh boots, making every step difficult and slow. He followed the general direction of the mountain road, not sure where to go. Everywhere the raging fire of the Cultural Revolution was burning. If he was caught, the guilty verdict and punishment against him would be doubled, and his death would be certain.

Gradually, his mind calmed down, and a thought rose in his mind, "I am innocent! I need to appeal to the government and protest for my freedom and right!"

He decided to go to Beijing to appeal at the Central Committee of the CCP State Council, the top authority of the government of the country. Strengthened by the thought, he also started walking much faster towards the capital city of the county where he would take the train to Beijing. . . .

At the Train Station

My father purchased a ticket for Beijing. But he had to wait another four hours for the next train. Inside the train station many people were waiting for their train, there were also red guards (Hong Weibing) and militiamen (Minbing) with red armbands everywhere. They walked back and forth to check people. They would check tickets and ask questions of any people they thought looked suspicious.

They were not police, but they had the exclusive authority to arrest anyone that might belong to the "monsters and freaks," also known as the "[Five] Black" categories—landowners, rightists, capitalists, etc., most of them educated intellectuals.

My father was hoping that after his long walk he could relax a little, and maybe get some sleep as he was extremely tired. But he realized he was not safe even in a big city far away from his home village. He tried his best to mingle in with groups of people, so he wouldn't be easy spotted by the red guards and militiamen. He also took off his eyeglasses as they too obviously gave him the appearance of an intellectual.

The station hall was cold and many people were smoking, making the air very bad. People all looked worried and nervous. No one was smiling. All over the station posters with revolutionary slogans were hung on walls, windows, and from the ceiling. Slogans such as:

"Carry Out the Great Proletarian Cultural Revolution to the End!"

"Sweep Away All the Monsters and Freaks!"

"Bury Capitalism!"

"The East Wind Blows, the Battle Drum Strikes, Now Who Is Afraid of Whom?"

"The Downfall of U.S. Imperialism Is Inevitable, the World's People Certainly Win!"

"Fight with Heaven, Earth, and People, and Reap Endless Enjoyment!"

Exhausted as he was, my father kept looking with sadness at the joyless expression of the people around him, and wondering what this "great" Cultural Revolution was really all about, and what good it was bringing to people.

Troubles at Home

Early the next morning, after my father had left, the head of the village militiamen came to our house to notify my father to be on time at the struggle session that night. When he realized my father wasn't home, he became upset and wanted to know where my father was. My mom was very nervous and said he had gone for a few days to see his aunt who had gotten very sick. So the man left. . . .

As my father had suddenly left home, there was nothing the village Cultural Revolution committee could do but cancel their scheduled struggle session. However, they were under great pressure from higher levels, and so they sent the militiamen to our house every day to ask when my father would be back. The man even carried a gun and talked in a loud and rude manner. Eventually he came several times a day, staying at our house longer and longer each day.

One day the head of the village came with several militiamen. He threatened my mom that he would take away our yearly grain rations if my father didn't come back. Taking away our grain rations meant that we would have nothing to eat. Peasants had no income. Even though they worked the entire year for the People's Commune Production Brigade, they were compensated at the end of the year with grain. But that was generally not enough to feed a family. Even if a farmer's family had several full-time adults working, the grain they earned was sometimes not enough to feed them all.

A family like ours could never earn enough food. As my father was labeled a counterrevolutionary, his full day work was worth only 70 percent of that of a regular laborer. My work, as a youth, was treated as half-labor, meaning for one day work I received half the number of work points compared to an adult—and only during the days of school breaks, when I could work. As a result, our family never had enough food. Only on Chinese New Year did my mom make a special meal of dumplings; and on my birthday she would boil two eggs, one for me and one for my sister. Such birthday treats were only for our grandmother and us kids; my parents never treated themselves.

As the head of the village Party branch said, if they really deducted all our food points, our whole year's work would be turned to nothing and our lives would be at risk. My mom became very angry and scared, but she could not talk back because if she said something that made him angry, they might arrest my mom or take her to the struggle session. Then there would be no one to take care of us. . . .

Every day we lived in fear. And while we were hoping that my father would be coming home soon, we were also afraid that if he did come back he would be tortured or killed by the village's Cultural Revolution leaders.

Returning to Tiananmen Square

Ma Jian

In the following viewpoint, Ma Jian reports on a visit to Tiananmen Square in Beijing in 2009, twenty years after the government violently ended demonstrations there. He took his young son with him and visited with acquaintances who remembered the crackdown. Ma notes that memories of the violence are still vivid for those who lived through it, although younger Chinese people are not particularly interested. Ma writes that Beijing has gone from being the site of oppression to becoming a major commercial center and the host of the 2008 Summer Olympic Games. Ma is a Chinese writer whose books include Stick Out Your Tongue, Beijing Coma, *and* The Noodle Maker.

Two thousand years ago, contemplating the relentless flow of time, [philosopher] Confucius gazed down at a river and sighed, "What passes is just like this, never ceasing day or night...." In China, time can feel both frozen and unstoppable at the same time. The Tiananmen massacre that 20 years ago ravaged Beijing, killed thousands of unarmed citizens, and altered the lives of millions, seems now to be locked in the 20th century, forgotten or ignored, as China continues to hurtle blindly towards its future.

The amnesia to which China has succumbed is not the result of natural memory-loss but of state-enforced erasure. China's Communist regime tolerates no mention of the massacre. But Tiananmen Square, and other sites connected with the events of 1989, still remain charged with memory. When the written and spoken word is censored, the urban landscape becomes a nation's only physical link to the past.

I left Beijing in 1987, shortly before my books were banned there, but have returned continually. In 1989, I was on Tiananmen Square with the students, living in their makeshift tents and joining their jubilant singing of the Internationale [a Communist song]. In the two decades since, each time that I have gone back, visions from those days seem to return with increasing persistence.

During the Beijing Olympics last August [2008], I took my now five-year-old son to the square. On our journey there, our movements were observed by the CCTV cameras in the lift [elevator] of our apartment block and outside the front gate from our compound, by the listening devices in our taxi, by the armed police who lined the streets and by the security guards who frisked us before finally allowing us on to Tiananmen. We emerged from the underpass and stepped on to the square. Apart from the crowds of policemen, the plain-clothes officers (instantly identifiable by their dark sunglasses and striped Airtex shirts) and the gaudy flower displays, the concrete-paved square, the size of nine football fields, was almost deserted.

In spring 1989, the square had been taken over by Beijing students and civilians who were mounting the largest peaceful protest in history. They were pressing for dialogue with their Communist leaders, and ultimately for freedom and democracy. The packed square became the city's pulsing heart; the police had vanished. This was a benevolent form of anarchy—noble, joyous, and surprisingly orderly.

Around the Square

My son ran to the spot where 20 years ago the students had erected a huge polystyrene replica of the Statue of Liberty. He looked northwards to Tiananmen Gate, the entrance to the Forbidden City where China's emperors used to live. In 1949, Mao stood on the gate and declared the founding of the People's Republic. Now the gate's blood-red walls were covered in scaffolding and green gauze. At politically sensitive times these walls are invariably covered for "important repair work", ensuring that the public won't get near enough to daub them with subversive slogans. The only bit of the gate that tourists could now photograph was the portrait of Chairman Mao over the central arch.

My son stared up at the tyrant's pink, pudgy face and asked me who he was. "Mao Zedong," I replied.

"Is he dead now?" he said, sweat dripping down his cheeks.

"He died years ago, his body is lying in that big building over there," I explained, pointing to the grey, concrete mausoleum behind us. My son turned round and ran off towards an ice-cream stall, and I thought of how, in 1989, I too had run across the square in the sweltering heat, with a bag of ice-lollies in my backpack, which I then handed out to my writer-friends who had marched to the square from the Lu Xun Writers' Academy, calling for freedom of expression and an end to government corruption. I gave them the victory sign as they paraded past. More than a million people were on the square that day. The sky was just as blue then, but instead of the scent of flowers and green turf, the air was filled with the sour smell of sweat, rotting refuse and exuberant cries of protest.

As my son peered into the vendor's ice box, I glanced at the bridge over the Jinshui moat that skirts Tiananmen Gate. It was now lined with police. They were there to prevent the suicide jumps of anti-government petitioners. Five years ago, a Beijinger named Ye Guoqiang had attempted just such a fatal jump as a protest against his recent and forceful eviction from his home in order to make way for an Olympic Games construction project.

He was sentenced to two years in prison for embarrassing the state. "If you want to kill yourself," the judge told him, "at least do it in the privacy of your own home, not beneath the Chairman's nose." Citizens can allow themselves to be shot dead by the army below Mao's portrait, but not to commit suicide there.

Opposite the Museum of Chinese History on the east side of the square, I took a photograph of my son standing in front of a garish maroon, yellow and orange potted flower display. The slogan above read: One World, One Dream. In early May 1989, during the students' mass hunger strike, I had told my friend that if the army came to the square and turned their guns on us, I would take her straight into the museum for cover. "You think they'd turn their guns on us?" she laughed. "Are you crazy?" She was wearing a straw hat at the time, with the words "Sorrow! Joy!" printed on the front. Like almost everyone else, she couldn't believe that the People's Liberation Army would shoot innocent civilians.

On May 28 1989, my brother had an accident in my home-town of Qingdao and fell into a coma. I immediately left Beijing to look after him, so I didn't witness the massacre of 4 June. (Perhaps if I had, I would never have been able to write about it.) My friend Li Lanju, the head of a Hong Kong student as-sociation, told me that in the early hours of 4 June she too had been sitting here in front of the museum. She saw PLA [People's Liberation Army] soldiers in green helmets pour out from inside and line up on the steps in front. A boy of about 15 ran towards the soldiers with a rock in his hand and shouted, "You just shot my brother! I want to avenge his death!" Li Lanju rushed over to him and pulled him back. But a few minutes later, a man ran past carrying the same boy in his arms. He was dead now, his face covered in blood. The Museum of Chinese History holds no records of those events that happened below its front steps.

I walked over to my son and bought him a panda-shaped ice cream on a stick. (Back in London, a month later, his mother and I were horrified to learn that the dairy products we'd been feeding him and his three-year-old sister had been contaminated with kidney-stone inducing melamine. The Chinese government had known that unscrupulous farmers had been adulterating milk to increase profit margins, but had suppressed all news of the scandal to avoid spoiling their Olympics propaganda pageant.)

From 1989's Massacre to 2008's Olympic Games

We continued south past Mao's mausoleum and my thoughts returned again to 1989, when a student in my tent told me how he longed to muster a few friends, charge into the mausoleum, drag out Mao's corpse and throw it into the Jinshui River. He said that as long as Mao's embalmed body remains in the square, China will have no peace.

Feeling tired and dispirited, I took my son's hand and led him across the road to the Qianmen district. In 1989, I'd often scarpered off to its crowded, bustling lanes in search of a quick bowl of noodles. Back then, stall holders would hand out free drinks and bread rolls to hungry protesters. I heard that after the students were driven out of the square on 4 June, street vendors came out with baskets of trainers [tennis shoes] to give to protesters who'd lost their shoes in the scrum. Today, the place was almost unrecognisable. In the run-up to the Olympics, the Ming Dynasty buildings along the main street, with their beautiful stone carvings and ornate wooden eaves, had been demolished and replaced by soulless, modern replicas of their former selves. I stood with my son amid the kitsch while locals wandered around in bewilderment, cameras in hand, now reduced to tourists in their own backstreets.

After a while, the sense of alienation from the past becomes suffocating and makes one long to reconnect with old friends. When I arrived in Beijing a few weeks before the Olympics, the secret police summoned me to the Sheraton Hotel and, over coffee and cakes, told me very politely not to speak in public, meet with any foreign journalists and especially to stay away from politically sensitive people such as Liu Xiaobo and Zhou

Duo—two of the four intellectuals who went on hunger strike in sympathy with the students during the last days of the democracy movement. Zhou Duo, a former economics professor at Beijing University, is an old friend of mine. He is a quiet, scholarly man, with a love of philosophy and classical music. In 1989 he became swept up in the democracy movement after the more flamboyant and charismatic essayist, Liu Xiaobo, declared him to be the most important intellectual of our generation. Zhou Duo had never taken much interest in politics before, so I was surprised to hear that he had joined the hunger strike. In the late hours of 3 June he and the Taiwanese rock star, Hou Dejian, went to negotiate with the army. While the students huddled in terror below the Monument to the People's Heroes, he implored the army to let the students retreat from the square in safety. His quiet, diplomatic demeanour no doubt saved thousands of lives.

Unlike Liu Xiaobo who, having spent several years in prison, is now in detention again for signing a charter last year calling for political reform, Zhou Duo has disappeared from public life. He hasn't been able to work or be published since 1989 and is under constant police surveillance. He regrets his involvement in the protests and the loss of his career. Having found God, he manages to hold small services in his heavily monitored flat in the outskirts of Beijing, and spends most of his time drawing up models for China's political future. Few will ever see them. We spoke briefly on his bugged phone before the Olympics, but I didn't dare suggest a meeting.

In February of this year I returned to China to research my next book. The authorities know about the novels of mine that have been published in the west, including the latest one, *Beijing Coma*, about a student shot in Tiananmen Square, but so far have allowed me to return. They continue to search me at customs, confiscate my documents and monitor my movements, but no doubt realise that as long as they deny me a voice in China, I can't do much harm. Although my next book has nothing to do

The books of Ma Jian, the author of this viewpoint, have been banned in China. © Ulf Andersen/Getty Images Entertainment/Getty Images.

with Tiananmen, a few days after my arrival in February I found myself involuntarily drawn back to that vast open space. I went there by taxi. The square was deserted and carpeted in snow. The emerald conifers along its perimeter drew one's gaze skyward. I wound down the window to take a photograph, but before I had time to press the shutter, the driver barked, "Close that window! There's a new rule, didn't you know? All taxi windows must be kept shut when driving past Tiananmen Square. It's been designated a 'politically sensitive area'."

This year is one of many important anniversaries in China, including the 60th of the founding of the People's Republic and the 20th of the Tiananmen massacre. The government is more on guard than ever. I wound up the window, glanced out at the square and recalled a multitude of raised hands, banners and flags. The cries of a million silenced protesters echoed in my mind's ear, saying more to me than anything my eyes could now see.

Beijing Coma took me 10 years to finish. The first few years, I wrote very little. A single recurrent image was blocking my progress: a man lying naked on an iron bed, a sparrow perched on his arm, his chest illuminated by a cold beam of light. Those 10 years were a struggle to prove to myself the power and meaning of that single beam of light.

"Why is it that men are so good at turning their heaven into a hell?" I muttered to myself as I closed my eyes.

The taxi driver looked out of his window and said, "That snow is nothing. You should see how much has fallen back in our village. . . ."

"I don't want to get out at the square any more," I said. "I've changed my mind. Please turn round and take me to Tongxian [a Beijing neighborhood]."

A Visit to a Controversial Friend

I had a sudden wish to visit the artist and photographer Chen Guang. The photographs he had taken many years ago of himself surrounded by naked women or having sex with a prostitute had been crude expressions of an inner rage. But recently, he had completed a series of oil paintings of the Tiananmen massacre, and had exhibited them on the internet.

I wanted to see them.

Chen Guang's flat in Tongxian is in an anonymous modern block. In the middle of his stark room was a plastic bucket filled with his cigarette stubs; the white walls were hung with green swirling paintings of tanks, helmeted soldiers and flattened tents. He gave me a glass of water and confessed that in 1989 he had joined the army. He was just 17. Within a few months of conscription, his regiment—number 62—was sent to Beijing to help quash the student movement. On 3 June his fellow soldiers received orders to disguise themselves as civilians, make their way independently to the Great Hall of the People on the west side of the square, and await the signal to drive the students out.

"There were 7,000 of us," he told me, lighting a new cigarette from the glowing stub of his last one, "and I was given the job of transporting our 4,000 assault rifles to the Great Hall. I dressed myself up as a student and loaded the guns on to a public bus the army had appropriated. As the driver edged through the packed crowds of students on Changan Avenue, I was terrified that they might jump up and spot the rifles stacked along the floor, so I leaned out and gave them a cheerful victory sign. When we reached the back yard of the Great Hall and locked the gates, I spent two hours unloading the guns, armful by armful. They were brand new. By the end, I was drenched in oil."

I'd never heard a soldier give a first-hand account of the crackdown. He took a deep drag from his cigarette and continued, his eyes beginning to redden: "Each soldier was given a loaded rifle and told to stand in line. Most of us were young boys from the villages. We had hardly eaten for days. We were weak and terrified, convinced we were going die. Some guys shat themselves, others were trembling so much that they inadvertently fired their guns and injured fellow soldiers.

A Soldier's Story

"At 12 midnight on 4 June the doors of the Great Hall were swung open. It was chaos outside. Special forces in camouflage were brandishing bayonets and driving out the students still left in the square. Nearby, a small group kicked a student to the ground and hit his skull with their rifle butts. I heard machine-gun fire in the distance, and saw the Goddess of Democracy being rammed by a tank and topple to the ground. . . .

"I clutched my rifle but didn't know where to point it. I was ordered to help clean the square and burn all evidence. I walked across the swath of flattened tents, blankets, sandals and leaflets, and picked up two journals and one long plait of black hair tied at the bottom with a plastic band. I guessed that some girl must have cut it off in despair before the army arrived. . . ."

I asked Chen Guang what was his most vivid memory of those days. He said, "After we sealed off central Beijing, we could go everywhere, places we'd never usually get to see. I remember wandering into the Zhongnanhai [the seat of government] compound. All the government leaders had abandoned their villas. Their pet cats and dogs were left to starve outside the front doors . . . I remember that, and other little details. But when I close my eyes and think back on those days, what I see first is the colour green, a nightmarish swirling green of helmets and tanks."

I told him that although I wasn't in Beijing during the crackdown, I too pictured a terrifying green, the sea of dehumanising khaki that kills and maims, when I came to describe those days in my book. I imagined how at dawn on 4 June, even the rising sun was stained green.

I asked him why he'd decided to talk about this now. "It's the 20th anniversary this year," he said. "I think it's about time. Anyway, I can't hold these nightmares inside me any longer." He is one of the few artists to have dared confront Tiananmen Square head-on. The day I met him, his internet exhibition was closed by the censors, just three days after going online.

Avoiding the Past

The Chinese have made a faustian pact with the government, agreeing to forsake demands for political and intellectual freedom in exchange for more material comfort. They live prosperous lives in which any expression of pain is forbidden. When I talk to young Chinese about 1989, I am invariably accused of spreading false rumours and being a traitor to my nation; when I bring up the subject with my old friends, most of them laugh scornfully, as if those events are now irrelevant. But I know that behind this show of derision or apathy lies real fear. Everyone knows that attempts to break the Tiananmen taboo can still destroy a person's life and the lives of their families. The authorities, for their part, may have a monopoly of the nation's resources, but they can never fully control the nation's soul, and every day they live in terror that the intricate stack of lies they have constructed will collapse.

Xidan Book Store, a five-minute walk down Changan Avenue from the Zhongnanhai government compound, is the largest bookshop in Asia. A few days after meeting Chen Guang, I went there to buy a Chinese translation of WG Sebald's *Austerlitz*. Like the protagonist, I too am always struggling to find out how many memories a human life needs. This five-floor bookshop sells 100,000 books a day. A huge poster of smiling President Obama is displayed close to the main entrance. Inside you can buy translations of the latest scientific or economic tomes, and books charting China's 5,000-year history, but you will not find a word about the Tiananmen massacre, or any accurate accounts of the other tragedies that the Communists have inflicted on China since 1949. These missing chapters of the nation's history weaken the power of every other Chinese text in the shop.

My mobile phone rang. I had arranged a meeting at the bookshop with Liu Hua, a Tiananmen survivor and son of a Beijing University professor. I glanced outside the window and knew at once that it was him. He was the only person in the crowd to have only one arm.

We walked together down Changan Avenue. A cold wind was blowing and the snow on the pavements had been shovelled towards a line of holly trees. The ancient red walls of the Zhongnanhai compound were glimmering in the evening sun. We reached the Liubukou intersection. A few years ago I'd stood here and taken photographs as part of my research for *Beijing Coma*. At that time, the gap between the eyewitness accounts I'd heard of the carnage that took place at this intersection in 1989 and the mundane reality before my eyes could not be closed without an effort of the imagination. Now, with Liu Hua right beside me, the present scene was instantly merged with the past. He had come on the dawn of 4 June with two young students.

A Victim Speaks

"It happened right here," he told me, "just by these white railings. A tank charged down Changan Avenue, and sprayed tear gas into the air. There was a big crowd of us. We were coughing and choking. We rushed on to the pavement, and I was squashed back against these railings. A girl dropped to her knees. I was grasping the railings with one hand to stop myself falling and with the other I offered her a handkerchief and told her to use it as a mask. Just as I was leaning over to hand it to her, another tank roared up and careered into us. Thirteen people were crushed to death but I only lost my arm. The tank commander knew exactly what he was doing." He stared down at the patch of asphalt at his feet and then glanced nervously at the police vans parked on the other side of the road. It was rush hour; cars and taxis were streaming past us.

"What a terrifying experience," I said, gripping the white railings.

"Yes, it was," he replied quite calmly. "But I wasn't truly afraid until I saw Deng Xiaoping on television, telling the martial law troops: 'Foreigners say that we opened fire, and that I admit, but to claim that army tanks drove over unarmed citizens, that is a disgraceful slur.' My scalp tightened. I was a living witness to the truth. What if one day they came to get me?. . . For two years I never dared go out at night, I never spoke about what happened. Policemen came to interrogate me almost every day, but none of us ever mentioned the tanks. Every anniversary of 4 June, the police would come to my house with pillows and mattresses and sleep on my bedroom floor. Just to stop me speaking to foreign journalists."

As the sun began to set, we retreated into a restaurant. I stared out at the darkening walls of the Zhongnanhai compound and thought of the government leaders inside sitting down for a family meal in their sumptuous villas, their cats and dogs scampering around their feet.

Liu Hua turned to me and said, "Those bloody Communists! What right did they have to take my arm from me? If they don't apologise for the crackdown and offer justice for the victims, I'll take them to the courts!"

Maintaining Hope

"Be sure to keep all your evidence and medical records safe," I said. "The day of reckoning is bound to come." I'm always surprised by how much faith the Chinese place in the legal system. In a country that has no rule of law, our only weapon in the fight for justice is the strength of our convictions.

Without these witnesses, we would become more and more distanced from the atrocity. In just 20 years, the Tiananmen generation that inspired people across the world to rise up against tyrannies has faded from view. School teachers, parents, newsreaders and armies of censors have collaborated in numbing a generation. It is left to brave survivors including Liu Hua, Chen Guang, and many others such as Ding Zilin, founder of the "Tiananmen Mothers" support group, to drag the dead back from oblivion and fight for truth.

Not all of those who died on 4 June did so unknowingly. Some chose deliberately to walk towards the rifles. As the bullets were flying towards them, possibly the one thought in their minds was: "This is the darkest moment; afterwards the light will come." The unfree bodies chose to fall so that millions of others could stand up freely again and trample on the injustices of the past. The only point of self-sacrifice is to force one's oppressors to live with the burden of guilt.

I think of my brother who 20 years ago fell into a coma. His wife and children abandoned him long ago. Today, he is able to eat, drink and sleep, but has no emotions or self-respect. He can't speak, but he can sit in front of a television show and laugh himself to tears. Or he can stare at the ceiling for hours on end. He has no control over his life. He is like the Chinese people.

And yet, something extraordinary happened the last time I visited him. I often give him a pen and paper and wait to see what he draws. Sometimes it's just boxes and crosses; sometimes he'll write my name or the name of his first girlfriend. But this time, he drew a picture of a horse galloping across an open field. Although the lines were shaky, they were more expressive than any I could have drawn. For a moment, I saw a faint beam of light on his chest, and I knew that there was still hope.

A Uighur Activist Recalls a Government Crackdown

Rebiya Kadeer

The Uighurs—Muslims living mostly in China's western Xinjiang province—are China's largest ethnic minority. They are provided representation in China's ruling organization, the National People's Congress. The following viewpoint is the account of one such representative, Rebiya Kadeer, following a visit to the city of Gulja in 1997. At the time, local protest demonstrations were put down by Chinese government forces, and Chinese authorities made it difficult to gather or release any information about the event. In Kadeer's account, the crackdown was one of extensive violence. Kadeer is a businesswoman who left for exile in the United States after several years in a Chinese prison. She is the president of the World Uyghur Congress.

I began hearing about terrible events occurring in Gulja in early February 1997, and decided—as a Uighur and a member of the Chinese National People's Congress, that I had to go to see for myself what was happening.

I arrived in Gulja City in the morning of February 7 or 8, and went to the home of a Uighur friend of mine. In the afternoon my friend took me to the home of another Uighur family whose two sons had been killed during the Chinese military crackdown on the peaceful protestors in Gulja a couple of days earlier. Their daughter had been arrested and her whereabouts were unknown. The parents were pale and highly distraught. Just as I was trying to talk with them, the Ili Prefectural Police and Chinese Military officers and soldiers burst into the house. The soldiers pulled the parents by the hair and kicked them really hard. The top military officer ordered me to put my hands on my head and to face the wall and said, "if you resist or shout and scream, we will shoot you." It was clear that it was the Chinese military officer in command, not the prefectural police, who didn't dare say anything in front of him. They forced me to strip completely naked and searched all my clothes.

After finding nothing I was ordered to put my clothes back on, and was taken to the prefectural police station for further questioning. The police chief warned me not to visit any more homes and to leave the city immediately. He said I would be held responsible for the deaths of any people I visited who passed information on to me, and even my own death if something terrible happened. I was then allowed to leave the police station. I nevertheless resolved to stay in the city to gather more information.

As I left the police station someone dropped a note in front of me which read "Go and visit the Yengi Hayat Neighbourhood." When I arrived in that neighbourhood I saw a large house with all the doors open, and even some food on the table, but with no one at home. I knocked at the house next door, but no one answered. I tried another house, and a Hui Muslim opened the door and addressed me in perfect Uighur. I asked him what had happened to the people in the house next door. He said they may have been killed in the demonstration. He said they had been really nice neighbours. When I asked him how many people had lived in the house he was not comfortable answering, but he said many had been killed in that neighbourhood and taken away in military trucks.

Help from Members of Other Minorities

I asked him if he could direct me to the home of a Uighur family in the neighbourhood, but he said most Uighurs would be too scared to let me into their homes. But he pointed me to the house of an Uzbek family. A 60-year-old Uzbek woman opened the door. Despite her concern that I was being followed she gave me some tea and spoke to me about the demonstration and the crackdown. She said she had seen numerous Chinese military trucks piled high with dead or beaten Uighurs going into the local Yengi Hayat Prison but had not seen people leaving. She said she was certain that nearly 1000 Uighurs had been taken into the prison, but that the prison could only accommodate 500 prisoners. Furthermore, she said she saw many military trucks leaving the prison that were filled with dirt. Many others I spoke with had also witnessed this. Many suspected that dead bodies were buried in the dirt and were being taken out to be disposed of.

Later, I visited the home of another individual, Abdushukur Hajim, who had not participated in the demonstration but who had witnessed killings by the Chinese military. While at his home, the Ili Prefectural Police broke in and detained me for a second time, again taking me back to the police station. I learned later that this gentleman was subsequently arrested and sentenced to two years in prison for passing "state secrets" to me. When he was released two years later he had had a mental breakdown.

Even after my second detention and warning by the Ili Prefectural Police I did not leave Gulja. I simply felt it was my responsibility to bear witness to the events there and to gather information. I was eventually detained a third time. When I arrived at the police station they said "we've told you repeatedly to leave but you are still here. OK, then, if you are so interested to know what happened here then look at this."

President of the World Uyghur Congress, Rebiya Kadeer, speaks at a Uyghur (also spelled as Uighur) protest in Washington, DC. © AP Images/Stephen J. Boitano.

A Film of the Attacks

They then showed me footage they had filmed of the military crackdown in Gulja in the proceeding days. I believe their intention was to terrify me and to intimidate me into silence. I watched the footage in the police station with several other people, including the prefectural police chief. I have never seen such viciousness in my life and it is difficult for me to adequately describe the horror of the scenes in the film. In one part dozens of military dogs were attacking—lunging and biting at peaceful demonstrators, including women and children. Chinese PLA [People's Liberation Army] soldiers were bludgeoning the demonstrators—thrashing at their legs until they buckled and fell to the ground. Those on the ground—some alive, others dead, were then dragged across the ground and dumped all together into dozens of army trucks.

The footage also captured a young Uighur girl screaming, "Semetjan", then running to a young man who was bleeding and being dragged by a Chinese soldier to a truck. Another soldier knocked her down and shot her dead right on the spot. He then dragged her by the hair and dumped her into the same truck into which the young man had been thrown. In another part of the film gunshots were fired into a group of Uighur children, aged 5 to 6, who were with a woman holding a baby, all were shot. It wasn't clear where the guns were being fired from, whether from a rooftop or truck-top. There were tanks in the street, and in the film one could see three kinds of PLA soldiers: those with a helmet, baton, and shield; those with automatic weapons; and those with rifles with bayonets. In the film I heard Chinese soldiers shouting, "kill them!, kill them!" I heard one officer shouting to a soldier, "Is he a Uighur or Chinese? Don't touch the Chinese but kill the Uighur."

After watching the footage I felt I had done what I could. I had seen enough of the horror. I left Gulja City for Urumchi. Upon arriving at the Gulja airport I was strip-searched by agents of the Chinese National Security Bureau. They confiscated all of my belongings, including my clothing and luggage. They gave me new clothing to wear and escorted me to the airplane.

Approximately ten days after my return to Urumchi, one woman and two young men from Gulja came to my office. They told me that they hadn't participated in the demonstration in Gulja but since the Chinese authorities [were] indiscriminately arresting many Uighurs, including those who hadn't participated in the demonstration, they decided to flee to Urumchi. One of them said his father was even a communist party member, but he still didn't feel safe. The woman told me with tears in her eyes that Chinese soldiers fired into a crowd of Uighurs waving goodbye to their relatives who were being paraded through the city streets in trucks on their way to the execution ground. She said when one desperate mother shouted to her son on the truck and raised her hands, Chinese soldiers on a building fired upon her with a machine gun and killed 5–6 Uighurs standing beside her. Some Russians standing nearby saw what happened and shouted "Fascists! Fascists!"

During my stay in Gulja I visited some 30 Uighur families and met with nearly 100 people. I felt the pain of the Uighur families who lost their sons and daughters in the military crackdown on this peaceful protest. Having been detained and threatened on three occasions, I was able to understand the severity of the situation by experiencing first hand mistreatment at the hands of Chinese military and police.

I am speaking out so that we do not forget those who lost their lives in Gulja and to call for accountability on the part of the Chinese authorities.

Glossary

backyard furnaces During the Great Leap Forward, Mao Zedong encouraged people's communes and in-town neighborhoods to maintain furnaces for steel production.

Central Committee of the Communist Party of China The ruling body in China. Its 350 members are chosen by the National People's Congress to serve five-year terms.

Communist Party of China (CPC) China's ruling party since the founding of the People's Republic in 1949. Also referred to as the Chinese Communist Party (CCP).

Cultural Revolution An attempt from 1966 to 1976 by China's leaders to overturn traditions and instill permanent revolutionary attitudes.

Democracy Movement The call by Chinese students and dissidents for political change that expanded throughout the 1980s and culminated in the Tiananmen Square demonstrations and crackdown in 1989.

General Secretary of the Communist Party of China China's leading official that is appointed by the ruling politburo.

Great Leap Forward China's attempt at rapid agricultural and industrial development from 1958 to 1962.

gulag A term for a prison or labor camp originally used in reference to Russia.

Hui A Muslim minority group in China.

Kuomintang The Chinese Nationalists who lost the nation's civil war to the Communist Party in 1949. They went on to govern Taiwan for many years.

Lower Mongolia A region of northern China mostly inhabited by ethnic Mongols.

National People's Congress (NPC) China's national representative body. It has little actual political power.

people's communes A form of collective farming that became an important feature of the Great Leap Forward. Private land ownership was abolished, and each commune was supposed to be self-sufficient and provide food for cities. At the movement's height in 1959, an estimate 125 million households lived on five thousand communes.

People's Liberation Army (PLA) China's national armed services. Also known as the Red Army.

politburo A core group of leaders chosen from the Central Committee of the Chinese Communist Party. It is generally understood to be the main political power in China.

Qinghai A region in northern China thought to contain many prison and labor camps.

Red Guards The foot soldiers of the first years of the Cultural Revolution, frequently high school or college students.

Tiananmen Square A large public square in Beijing, China's capital city.

Tibet A formerly independent state in Western China, now known as Xizang.

Uighurs One of China's largest ethnic minorities. The Uighurs speak a language related to Turkish and are mostly Muslims. Also spelled Uyghurs.

Xinjiang province A territory in western China largely inhabited by Uighurs. Uighur activists consider it part of "Greater Turkestan" in Central Asia.

Organizations to Contact

The editors have compiled the following list of organizations concerned with the issues debated in this book. The descriptions are derived from materials provided by the organizations. All have publications or information available for interested readers. The list was compiled on the date of publication of the present volume; the information provided here may change. Be aware that many organizations take several weeks or longer to respond to inquiries, so allow as much time as possible.

Amnesty International
5 Penn Plaza, 16th Floor
New York, NY 10001
(212) 807-8400
website: www.asiapacific.amnesty.org

Amnesty International is a global human rights organization. The Asia/Pacific division deals with such matters as the arrest and imprisonment of dissidents and protesters in China.

Chinese Human Rights Defenders
PO Box 1905
Washington, DC 20013
website: www.crhdnet.com

Based in China, Chinese Human Rights Defenders is a network that collects information on human rights abuses in China and inspires activism against such abuses.

Congressional-Executive Commission on China (CECC)
243 Ford House Office Building
Washington, DC 20515
(202) 226-3766 • fax: (202) 226-3804
website: www.cecc.gov/index.php

Created by the US Congress in 2000, the CECC is charged with monitoring human rights and the development of the rule of law in China. The commission is comprised of nine senators, nine members of the House of Representatives, and five senior administration officials appointed by the president. The commission prepares an annual report, available on its website, as well as other publications including issue papers and the CECC newsletter. The website also includes a database of political prisoners in China and a Virtual Academy, which includes extensive information on China in general.

Human Rights in China (HRIC)
HRIC New York Office
350 Fifth Ave., Suite 3311
New York, NY 10118
(212) 239-4495
website: www.hrichina.org

Human Rights in China was founded by pro-reform protesters in 1989 during the lead-up to the demonstrations in Tiananmen Square. It seeks to expand the rule of law in China, find ways to provide institutional protection for human rights, and pressure China to adhere to international human rights agreements.

Human Rights Watch
350 5th Ave., 34th Floor
New York, NY 10118-3299
(212) 290-4700
website: www.hrw.org

Human Rights Watch is an advocacy and lobbying group with offices around the world. Its efforts in China focus on alleged human rights abuses including the abuse of workers, mistreatment of ethnic minorities, and imprisonment of dissidents.

Montreal Institute for Genocide and Human Rights Studies (MIGS)
Concordia University
1455 De Maisonneuve Blvd. West
Montreal, Quebec, H3G 1M8 Canada
(514) 848-2424, ext. 5729 or 2404 • fax: (514) 848-4538
website: http://migs.concordia.ca

MIGS, founded in 1986, monitors native-language media for early warning signs of genocide in countries deemed to be at risk of mass atrocities. The institute houses the Will to Intervene (W2I) Project, a research initiative focused on the prevention of genocide and other mass atrocity crimes. The institute also collects and disseminates research on the historical origins of mass killings and provides comprehensive links to this and other research materials on its website.

STAND/United to End Genocide
1025 Connecticut Ave., Suite 310
Washington, DC 20036
(202) 556-2100
e-mail: info@standnow.org
website: www.standnow.org

STAND is the student-led division of United to End Genocide (formerly Genocide Intervention Network). STAND envisions a world in which the global community is willing and able to protect civilians from genocide and mass atrocities. In order to empower individuals and communities with the tools to prevent and stop genocide, STAND recommends activities from engaging government representatives to hosting fundraisers, and has more than one thousand student chapters at colleges and high schools. While maintaining many documents online regarding genocide, STAND provides a plan to promote action as well as education.

United Human Rights Council (UHRC)
104 N. Belmont Street, Suite 313
Glendale, CA 91206
(818) 507-1933
website: www.unitedhumanrights.org

The United Human Rights Council (UHRC) is a committee of the Armenian Youth Federation. The UHRC works toward exposing and correcting human rights violations of governments worldwide. The UHRC campaigns against violators in an effort to generate awareness through boycotts, community outreach, and education. The UHRC website focuses on the genocides of the twentieth century.

World Uyghur Congress
PO Box 310312, 80103
Munich, Germany
0049 (0) 89 5432 1999
website: www.uhygurcongress.org

The World Uyghur Congress is an organization based in Europe. It seeks to create unity among and awareness of all people with a Uyghur heritage, including the many living in Xinjiang province or elsewhere in China. The group partly emerged in response to the oppression of Uyghurs in China.

List of Primary Source Documents

The editors have compiled the following list of documents that either broadly address genocide and persecution or more narrowly focus on the topic of this volume. The full text of these documents is available from multiple sources in print and online.

Bangkok Declaration, 1993

Asian nations declare their support for international agreements and standards for human rights while recognizing the need for respect of the sovereignty and distinct values of independent states.

Charter 08, 2008

In 2008 a group of Chinese intellectuals and activists published a statement calling for greater recognition of human rights and democratic reforms.

Communique of the Fourth Plenary Session of the Central Committee of the Communist Party of China, 1979

Chinese leaders acknowledge that the country is in transition from the upheaval of the years of Mao Zedong's leadership (1949–1976) to the "four modernizations" of the future (building up agriculture, industry, national defense, and science and technology).

Constitution of the People's Republic of China, 1982

China's government recognized in 1982 the troubles that came along with the creation of a Communist state but reasserted that the establishment of a Communist China was its goal nevertheless. The constitution recognizes individual and ethnic rights and affirms overall state control of the economy.

Convention Against Torture and Other Cruel, Inhuman or Degrading Treatment or Punishment
United Nations, 1974

The United Nations General Assembly created a draft resolution in 1974 opposing any nation's use of torture, unusually harsh punishment, or unfair imprisonment.

Convention on the Prevention and Punishment of the Crime of Genocide, 1948

This resolution by the United Nations General Assembly defines genocide in legal terms and advises participating countries to prevent and punish actions of genocide in war and peacetime.

Principles of International Law Recognized in the Charter of the Nuremberg Tribunal
United Nations International Law Commission, 1950

After World War II (1939–1945) the victorious allies legally tried surviving leaders of Nazi Germany in the German city of Nuremberg. The proceedings established standards for international law that were affirmed by the United Nations. Among other standards, national leaders can be held responsible for crimes against humanity, which might include "murder, extermination, deportation, enslavement, and other inhuman acts."

Rome Statute of the International Criminal Court, 1998

The treaty that created the International Criminal Court establishes the court's functions, jurisdiction, and structure.

United Nations General Assembly Resolution 96 on the Crime of Genocide, 1946

This resolution by the United Nations General Assembly affirms that genocide is a crime under international law.

Universal Declaration of Human Rights, 1948

The United Nations approved this general statement of individual rights that would apply to citizens of all nations.

Whitaker Report on Genocide, 1985

This report addresses the question of the prevention and punishment of the crime of genocide. It calls for the establishment of an international criminal court and a system of universal jurisdiction to ensure that genocide is punished.

White Paper on China's Ethnic Policy and Common Prosperity and Development of All Ethnic Groups, 2009

The Information Office of the State Council of the People's Republic of China released an official statement on China's policy of equality concerning ethnic minority groups as well as respect for their religions and traditions.

White Paper on Human Rights in China, 1991

The Information Office of the State Council of the People's Republic of China released an official statement asserting the rights of individuals in the People's Republic as well as the progress of the Chinese state in protecting human rights. It notes China's advancing prosperity as the foundation of human rights.

For Further Research

Books

Stephen Angle and Marina Svensson, eds., *The Chinese Human Rights Reader: Documents and Commentary*. Armonk, NY: Sharpe, 2002.

Jasper Becker, *Hungry Ghosts: Mao's Secret Famine*. New York: Holt Paperbacks/Macmillan, 1998.

Ian Buruma, *Bad Elements: Chinese Rebels from Los Angeles to Beijing*. New York: Random House, 2001.

Anita Chan, Richard Madsen, and Jonathan Unger, *Chen Village Under Mao and Deng*. Berkeley: University of California Press, 1992.

Frank Dikötter, *Mao's Great Famine: The History of China's Most Devastating Catastrophe*. New York: Walker and Company, 2010.

John K. Fairbank, *The Great Chinese Revolution, 1800–1985*. New York: Harper and Row, 1986.

A.D.W. Forbes, *Warlords and Muslims in Chinese Central Asia*. Cambridge, UK: Cambridge University Press, 1986.

Rob Gifford, *China Road: Journey into the Future of a Rising Power*. New York: Random House, 2008.

Stanley Karnow, *Mao and China: A Legacy of Turmoil*. New York: Penguin, 1990.

Philip A. Kuhn, *The Origins of the Modern Chinese State*. Stanford, CA: Stanford University Press, 2002.

Fang Lizhi, *Bringing Down the Great Wall: Writings on Science, Culture, and Democracy in China*. New York: W.W. Norton, 1992.

Colin Mackerras, *China's Minorities: Integration and Modernization in the Twentieth Century*. Hong Kong: Oxford University Press, 1995.

Harrison E. Salisbury, *The New Emperors: China in the Era of Mao and Deng*. New York: Little, Brown, 1992.

Harrison E. Salisbury, *Tiananmen Diary: Thirteen Days in June*. Boston: Little, Brown, 1989.

Orville Schell, *Mandate of Heaven*. New York: Simon and Schuster, 1994.

Michael D. Schoenhals, ed., *China's Cultural Revolution, 1966–69*. Armonk, NY: Sharpe, 1996.

Harry Wu and Carolyn Wakeman, *Bitter Winds: A Memoir of My Years in China's Gulag*. New York: Wiley, 1994.

Mok Chiu Yu and J. Frank Harrison, eds., *Voices from Tiananmen Square: Beijing Spring and the Democracy Movement*. Armonk, NY: Sharpe, 1990.

Periodicals and Internet Sources

Audra Ang, "Tiananmen 20 Years Later: A Survivor's Story," Associated Press/ABC News, April 11, 2009.

Christopher Boden, "China Responds to Inner Mongolia Unrest by Deploying Force and Barring Protesters from Gathering," *Huffington Post*, June 1, 2011.

Shirong Chen, "China Tightens Internet Censorship Controls," BBC News, May 4, 2011.

"Why Good Intentions May Lead to Turmoil and Riot," *China Daily*, June 23, 1989.

Gregory Clark, "The Tiananmen Square Massacre Myth," *Japan Times*, September 15, 2004.

Peter Foster et al., "Teenage Daughter of Missing Chinese Dissident Appeals to Barack Obama," *Telegraph* (UK), October 28, 2010.

Tom Lasseter, "Four Decades Later, China Still Isn't Discussing Cultural Revolution," McClatchy Newspapers, August 24, 2010.

Mark Mackinnon, "Profiles in Courage: China's Dissident Gang of 10," *Globe and Mail* (Toronto), December 3, 2010.

David Mehegan, "A Child's View of the 'Great Leap,'" *Taipei Times*, June 15, 2008.

Andrew J. Nathan, "The Tiananmen Papers," *Foreign Affairs*, January–February 2001.

"The Red Guards: Today, China; Tomorrow, the World," *Time*, September 23, 1966.

Other

China News (www.china.org.cn). This general website featuring news from China is continually updated.

Chinese Posters (www.chineseposters.net). This website provides examples of propaganda posters used by the Chinese government to promote such policies as the Great Leap Forward and the Cultural Revolution.

Morning Sun (www.morningsun.org). This website is maintained by the makers of a film about the Cultural Revolution. It provides links to many original documents and images.

People's Daily (www.english.peopledaily.com.cn). This Chinese government and newspaper website provides resources on the general study of China and discussion forums.

Tiananmen: The Gate of Heavenly Peace (www.tsquare.tv). This website provides a comprehensive look at the pro-democracy protests in Tiananmen Square in Beijing in 1989 as well as the violent crackdown. It supplies photographs, written accounts, updates on participants, and related events.

To Live (1994). This film tells the story of a married couple struggling to survive the dramatic changes occurring in Communist China.

Xiu Xiu, The Sent Down Girl (1998). This film is about a young teenage girl who, as part of the Cultural Revolution, is sent to a remote area of China in 1975 to do manual labor.

Index